PARENTING SCRIPTS

When What You're Saying Isn't Working, Say Something New

Wendy Speake and Amber Lia

Endorsements:

"What a beautiful, beautiful, helpful offering Wendy and Amber give us in *Parenting Scripts*. I love it. The whole thing: the idea, the Scripts based on Scripture, the hope, and the encouragement. If you're struggling with your words, I highly recommend *Parenting Scripts*."

~ Sarah Mae, author of
Desperate: Hope for the Mom Who Needs to Breathe

"If you loved *Triggers* by Wendy Speake and Amber Lia, you are going to flip for their follow-up book, *Parenting Scripts*. This is a busy mom's best friend, packed full of practical help, including actual scripts to say when you are triggered."

~ Heidi St. John, author of
Becoming Mom Strong and the
Becoming Mom Strong Bible Study,
host of The Busy Mom podcast

If *Triggers* was a lighthouse, shining like a beacon of hope for parents flailing on the turbulent seas of angry reactions, *Parenting Scripts* is now the much-needed lifeboat, providing practical in-the-water help for fledgling parents. Each script is a lifeline that buoys parents out of their unproductive communication habits and equips them with life-giving words. Even the most seasoned parents can feel adrift in the wild waters of raising spirited kids. More stable ground is possible! *Parenting Scripts* is your guide to get there.

~ Becky Keife, writer, speaker,
editorial coordinator for (in)courage,
and mom of three spirited boys

"I don't want to yell at my kids. But in the heat of the moment, I can't think of any other way to manage the chaos of my four energetic boys. That was until Wendy Speake and Amber Lia, took the time to write out *Parenting Scripts*. Now instead of heading to my default response, I have a better alternative. And a prayer script to invite God to work on my boys from the inside out."

~Heather MacFadyen,
host of the GodCenteredMom Podcast
and grateful mom

"Practical, helpful, and biblical. Amber and Wendy have packed *Parenting Scripts* with solid, common sense, proven wisdom. Parents, give yourself a time-out and read this powerful book. It will lower your stress and frustration and raise your hope and enjoyment!"

~Pam Farrel, co-director of Love-Wise,
author of forty-four books including,
10 Best Decisions a Parent Can Make

"Are you a parent desperate for help? If you're stuck in bad parenting practices that weigh you down with fear and regret then *Parenting Scripts* offers real help to reset the negative voice in your head and break free from bad parenting habits that have you feeling guilty and overwhelmed. This book is an easy read that offers practical steps toward real and positive change by training parents to re-script the negative voice in your head while offering ways to speak words that affirm, inspire and guide your kids toward maturity. And if you apply the biblical principles laid out in this book, don't be surprised if you're the one who matures!"

~ Rhonda Stoppe, author of
Moms Raising Sons to Be Men

"Ever wish motherhood came with a manual? Stop wishing and run to buy this book! *Parenting Scripts* is the book I wished for when I became a mother back in 2008. With four children who span infancy through age nine, I have no doubt I will be keeping this book close at hand. Through Scripture, prayer prompts, and real-life examples, Amber Lia and Wendy Speake have created an invaluable resource for parents who want to biblically parent their children through every scenario possible. *Parenting Scripts* is a must-have for every mom."

~Erin Odom, author of
More Than Just Making It
and creator of thehumbledhomemaker.com

"Parenting Scripts is soaked in godly wisdom, and it will no doubt challenge you to rethink how you respond to your children. Wendy and Amber provide a gateway to freedom through gentle mentoring with their practical scripts for those of us who struggle with less-than-great responses to our little darlings."

~ Katie Bennett, author of
Heavenly Minded Mom
and creator of Embracing a Simpler Life

"*Parenting Scripts* is the resource I needed ten years ago when the stress of a difficult, strong-willed second child left me bewildered, not just by my child's behavior, but by my adverse natural reactions to it and my cluelessness as to how to handle it in a godly way. By God's grace we made it through, but *Parenting Scripts* will undoubtedly make all the difference for today's well-intentioned moms who need help responding to their child's unique needs and behaviors."

~ Jenny Rapson, editor of ForEveryMom.com

"When I read the first chapter of *Parenting Scripts* aloud to my husband he said, 'What? Do they live in our house?' Amber and Wendy get it. They understand the real, the hard, and the crazy you are immersed in as you're trying your best to raise up your tiny humans. If you want practical, specific, doable, grace-filled guidance to help you respond to your kid's daily mayhem in a Christlike way, *Parenting Scripts* is for you."

~ Elise Hurd, faith coach
and creator of littlelunchmaker.com

"Would you like new way to reach the heart of your child? Then grab a copy of *Parenting Scripts*, by Wendy Speake and Amber Lia. These mamas gracefully convey how you can change your parenting approach in order to speak life and truth to your child using carefully thought-out and customizable parenting scripts. The scripts are entirely inspired by Scripture as well as the vision for who you want your child to become. If words don't come easy to you or if you're caught in a negative cycle of empty threats and harsh words, I encourage you to learn from the wisdom of these moms. It's an investment you won't regret."

~ Elisa Pulliam, author of
Meet the New You: A 21-Day Plan of Embracing Fresh Attitudes and Focused Habits for Real Life Change, ImpactTogether, Biblical Mentoring Simplified, and founder of MoretoBe.com

"Our words have power. They can teach or they can crush. They can guide, or they can express all our frustration and anger. We can complain, or we can turn to God and ask Him to guide our tongues. As a mom of ten, I often find myself struggling with what to say when one of my kids is acting out. I love Amber Lia and Wendy Speake's practical approach: decide on your words during calm moments so they flow naturally during moments of conflict. This book is a perfect tool for parents who feel they're at their whit's end. With a strong, Scriptural foundation, parents can discover new ways to train their children toward righteousness by using the right words at the right time. Highly recommended!"

~ Tricia Goyer, USA Today best-selling
author of seventy books, including
*Walk It Out: The Radical Result
of Living God's Word One Step at a Time*

"What a powerful and practical resource! No matter where you are in your parenting journey, you'll glean so much wisdom from these pages. The beauty of *Parenting Scripts* is that Wendy and Amber don't simply tell us how we *should* respond to our children—which is always so much harder in the heat of the moment. But they give actual handrails to guide us through our responses, equipping us to be intentional parents rather than reactionary ones."

~ Kat Lee, author of
Hello Mornings and founder of HelloMornings.org

What Parents are saying about Parenting Scripts:

"As a mom, I like to appear like I've got it all together. 'Look at me! My children are polite, cheerful, smiling, and they have their shirts tucked in!' What I don't want to show you are those too-frequent moments when with clenched teeth I'm threatening my unruly children with deportation to the Artic Circle *sohelpmeGod*. *Parenting Scripts* is a lifeline in choppy parenting waters. Through the pages of this book, I realize the redemptive power of God in my home begins with His goodness to me. Grab up a copy of this book, and run home to read it. Clasp onto the love and mercy found in every single page and revel in the freedom of a home filled with beauty and truth. I'll be right here with you, re-reading my copy too."

~ Bethany Hockenbury,
mom of three (St. Louis, MO.)

"So many times parents get into a rut of saying things out of habit. Amber and Wendy have done a beautiful job reminding parents it's okay to have a do-over. Then they equip us with actual scripts based on Scriptures."

~ Jenn McClure,
mom of four (Austin, TX.)

"What sets *Parenting Scripts* apart from every other parenting book out there is how applicable it is. Every page is encouraging and helpful! Now I am seeing all of our stressful family challenges as opportunities to parent better with intentional, well thought-out responses."

~ Jacqui Miranda,
mom of four (Beaverton, OR)

"I know I need to be gentle. I know I need to speak life, but I've been so deep in generational bondage I'm simply not able been able to form gentle life-giving words in stressful moments. *Parenting Scripts* is teaching me to plan for those anger-making triggers ahead of time. I love this resource! Even in the chapters and situations where my circumstances are different than those presented in this book, the heart of the matter is the same. I have been able to take the vocabulary Amber Lia and Wendy Speake use to respond lovingly to my husband and my children. This book is retraining my mind and my heart and from there my mouth. I've prayed for years, 'Lord teach me what I am to say. Give me wisdom.

Show me a different way." *Parenting Scripts* has been a very real answer to that prayer."

~ Alexis MacPhee,
mom of four (Ontario, Canada)

"I am so grateful for Wendy Speake and Amber Lia and their books. Both *Triggers* and now *Parenting Scripts* are full of real, applicable help. These books have changed my life. And I'm pretty sure they'll change generations of my family to come. Hopefully my sons will step off the crazy wheel I created and put Wendy and Amber's directions into place in their families. Not just directions, but specific words for specific situations. I'm grateful."

~ Sherry Murrow,
mom of two (Centennial, CO)

Dedication:

To our boys: Caleb, Brody, & Asher; Oliver, Quinn, Oakley, & Quade, you have graciously allowed us to learn gentleness by your side, & share the stories here ... we love you.

TABLE OF CONTENTS

Introduction

Wendy

What do your children do each day that never fails to take you by surprise, wishing you had responded with different words and, perhaps, a different tone? When you can put your finger on what those recurring trouble spots are, there's a chance you just might be able to slow down, sit down, and write down a better response.

After we wrote our first book, *Triggers: Exchanging Parents' Angry Reactions for Gentle Biblical Responses,* letters started flooding in. "But what should I say when my child does x, y, and z?" They give us scenarios, ranging from toddler tantrums and teenage defiance, to selective hearing and homework meltdowns. "Tell me what to say when my kids …"

We respond to many of them online, with short posts we call "PARENTING SCRIPTS." This book is a collection of our favorite ones.

While Amber and I certainly don't always say and do the right things as moms, we are passionate about not continuing to say and do the same wrong things day after day. Einstein is credited for saying, "The definition of insanity is doing the same thing over and over and expecting different results."

Yes, we can get caught in this crazy-making cycle at home as well.

Climbing our way out of these well-worn ruts is the main goal of this book. If you and your family are stuck, speaking the same old words of correction to no avail, might we suggest you try different words?

But what words?

While there are no one-size-fits-all answers, we do believe in the power of conversation. This book is intended to spark a dialogue. We share some of our thoughts with you, even a possible "Parenting Script," and then you respond by talking it through with God and, ideally, your spouse. Finally, you'll get to write down your own plans for what you'll say the next time your child does that thing they always do.

Are you consistently taken by surprise when your children do the same wrong behaviors day after day? And are you shocked by the same explosive responses that tumble out over your lips? This book is your place to craft a better response for next time, because there will be a next time—I guarantee.

When parents write their letters asking for our help, our response to these brave men and women almost always starts with praise, because they are confessing to doing wrong and want desperately to do right. Next, we throw out a suggestion or two that we may have tried ourselves. However, we're always sure to tell them, "… these are simply suggestions to get you thinking outside of the confining box you may be parenting in. You don't have to do or say what we suggest, but you do have to do something different if what you're doing isn't working or is unkind." We will be careful to remind you of this as well in the chapters ahead. These are merely suggestions intended to inspire you.

Each child, each parent, and each home, when mixed together, makes up its own unique brand of family—that requires you to discover your own answers. Which is why, at the end of each chapter, we've included a section titled "Make the Script Your Own."

We're here to inspire you with some of our stories, to share some thought-provoking Scriptures and prayers, and to offer you ample space in our Workbook Pages (beginning on page 239) to write yourself a new script.

Chapter 1 —
Before You Say
Anything Else

Wendy

Parenting can be overwhelming. Some days are especially rough. But when those rough days start rolling seamlessly together, one right into the next without end, moms and dads feel hopeless. The kids do too! You're exhausted, your spouse is exhausted, even the children know there's something wrong. Trouble is, you don't know how to stop the cycle of exasperated sighs and negative correction.

Heading out the door for school, your biggest kid melts down over having to wear his jacket. Dropping him off, he discovers he left his backpack and lunch at home. Taking the younger kids to the park, the toddler throws a tantrum over not getting a specific sand toy. Eventually you carry them all, one limp body at a time, back to the car and home again where they refuse to eat what's served for lunch, then fight their way through naps. At dinner, your spouse gets angry and storms off, leaving you alone with emotional kids. It's the end of another long day, but there's still homework to get through and a sink full of dishes. An hour later, the toddler makes her way out of bed for the umpteenth time. "I need another glass of water," she whimpers from the shadows of the hallway. When all is finally said and done and you're on your way to bed, you decide to check your email one more time, only to find another note from your middle child's teacher communicating everything he did wrong that day ...

Where in the world does a parent start fixing problems, Where in the world does a parent start fixing problems, when it feels like everything and everyone is the problem? Today we begin at the beginning.

when it feels like everything and everyone is the problem? "In the beginning, God ..." (Genesis 1:1)

Let that settle in your bones.

The first four words of the Bible tell us God was there in the beginning. Before He created the heavens and the earth, there was God. Before He created the first man and the first woman and the first family, there was God. God pronounced the family—and all things He made—as good. Trouble is, it's also hard. But good things are often hard things, and hard things propel us to call on our good God for His help. So that's where we find ourselves at the beginning of this book: asking for help.

Here at the start of this chapter we're going to begin with a Prayer Script. From this point forward, however, Prayer Scripts will be found at the end of each chapter. But today it only seems right to start by calling out for help.

PRAYER SCRIPT:

Dear Lord, I need Your help. Some of my words haven't been working. Many of them haven't been working. I need Your Words instead. Your Words to instruct me and Your Words tumbling out over my lips instead of my own. Yes, Lord, I'm starting with this simple confession: What I'm doing isn't working, and I need Your help. You promise that when we seek You with all our heart, we'll find You. That's what I'm doing here at the start of this book. Let me find You in the days and pages ahead. Shine Your Word like a light on my parenting path, that I might have wisdom about what to say and what to do, so that my children don't just grow to honor me … but grow to honor and obey You. I need You, Holy Spirit. You are my Helper, and I am in sore need of help. Thank you for inclining Your ear to me and coming to my rescue. And Lord, while I'd love to see you transform the little people in my home, it's okay if you want to start with me. In Jesus' Name, amen.

The first gift I received after my husband Matt and I were engaged was a book entitled, *The Power of a Praying Wife* by Stormie Omartian. My friend Summer gave it to me in a little white gift bag. As soon as she left my home that spring day I opened the book, eager to cover my fiancé in prayer. Surprised, I found instead that the first chapter had nothing at all to do with my future husband and everything to do with his future wife. Before I could prayerfully support him, I had to start with me, confessing my own need for God's intervening help.

The same is true here.

Do our children do wrong day after day? Absolutely, but our job isn't to get so focused on their behavior that we lose sight of our own, so focused on their hearts that we don't invite the Lord to do a work in ours. Though their immaturity challenges us, the Lord is much more concerned with our own maturity. After all, we're the adults. We're the parents. If we want to turn things around in our home, the best place to start is always by bringing ourselves humbly to the throne of grace where transformation happens. "In the beginning, God …" Offer Him complete access to your family—through the doorway of your own surrendered life.

The fruit may be slow-growing in their lives, but it is growing. This includes the fruit of self-control and brotherly kindness, along with their ability to come to the table when called. Dear moms and dads, I know that you can get all stressed out each day, wondering when they will show you respect, brush their teeth, and be able to get their shoes on without melting down, but that day is coming. Today, however, I want to encourage you to turn your gaze from your children's immaturity to your own maturing process. Invite the Lord of heaven and earth to speak to your heart about your own fit-throwing tendencies. Ask God to grow you up to look more like Him and less like them!

Trust me on this one. As He deals with your slow-growing fruit, your children will be watching and learning from your transforming example. Don't join your children in their immature struggles, but gently and consistently invite them to join you in maturity.

> *... until we all attain to the unity of the faith, and of the knowledge of the Son of God, to a mature man, to the measure of the stature which belongs to the fullness of Christ. As a result, we are no longer to be children, tossed here and there by waves and carried about by every wind of doctrine, by the trickery of men, by craftiness in deceitful scheming; but speaking the truth in love, we are to grow up in all aspects into Him who is the head, even Christ ... (Ephesians 4:13-15, NASB).*

You are willing to change! We know you are. You're willing to repent, forgive, and be forgiven. You're willing to be refined and be transformed. You're willing to learn a whole new way of communicating with your people, from the littlest to the biggest, so let's get going.

Let's start with ourselves: "Search me, O God, and know my heart; Try me and know my anxious thoughts; And see if there be any hurtful way in me, And lead me in the everlasting way" (Psalm 139:23-24, NASB). Speak these words to the Lord before you speak to your kids, and He just might help you write a better response to whatever it is that's making you lose your temper and join them in their immaturity. Remember the parable in Matthew 7 about the man who needs to remove the log in his own eye before focusing on the speck in his brother's? That's what we're doing here.

PARENTING SCRIPT:

If you have been doing things wrong—shaming and blaming, using unkind words and short-tempered responses, or simply letting behavior (theirs and yours) go unchecked for far too long—it's time to make a better plan. When you are ready to apply some new plans and speak your new scripts, we suggest you start with this one:

"Hey kids, I want to take a moment to apologize. I'm sorry for some of the things I've been saying and doing in our home. I'm going to be doing and saying a few things differently from here on out. I might forget sometimes and make mistakes, and I know you'll make some mistakes too, but I want to talk with you the way God talks with me. God is gentle with me and longsuffering too, He builds me up and doesn't tear me down. Would you forgive me for the mistakes I've made? I'm so happy God gave you to me. And I'm so grateful for forgiveness."

In our family we have occasional "come to Jesus meetings" where we talk about our family's values and behavior at the end of our most difficult days and make plans for a bright tomorrow, full of new mercies. Schedule a meeting with your family, but first take a moment to write out what you want to say. Perhaps you need to apologize for teaching your kids to only answer you when you yell. Apologize for that, and let them know that things are going to be changing. Invite them to join you in the transformation process. If you have a spouse, go to him or her first and invite him/her to partner in this with you.

"How good and pleasant it is when God's people live together in unity" (Psalm 133:1, NIV)!

Here at the beginning, together ask God to give you a shared vision for your parenting and jot down ideas about what that may look like.

SCRIPT-URE:

"Search me, O God, and know my heart;
Try me and know my anxious thoughts;
And see if there be any hurtful way in me,
And lead me in the everlasting way"
(Psalm 139:23-24, NASB)

MAKE THE SCRIPT YOUR OWN:

All the other chapters will focus on specific issues in your home and encourage you to pen a gentle response in a moment void of conflict. In this chapter, however, we invite you to ask God what He wants to say to you before you say another word to your kids. In the workbook pages, spend some time listening and then write a script confessing where you've fallen short. Finally, invite your family to join you in this transforming journey. Perhaps you'll feel led to hold a "come to Jesus meeting" of your own.

Chapter 2 —
When Your Child Needs
Positive Motivation

Amber

The afternoon was in full swing. The four year olds had made it through a retelling of Noah's ark, complete with flannel graph animals, and they anxiously awaited snack time as they eyeballed the pink and white frosted cookies dotted with sprinkles. The class was a well-oiled machine. The Sunday school teacher was no rookie. She escorted each team to their tables and spritzed their hands with sanitizer before saying a brief prayer of thanksgiving.

After snack time, the four year olds cleared their tables as quickly as they could, stacking papers, cramming nubby crayons into their boxes, and sitting up straight like good soldiers.

"The penguin table can line up."

"The polar bears can line up."

"The rhinos still need to wipe down their table a little more, and then they can line up."

One by one, the children hurried to the line that led to an outdoor paradise of sand toys, jungle gyms, and footballs. They shuffled from one worn sneaker to the other in anticipation. And then the teacher said it: "When we go outside we are *not* going to:

Throw sand.

Push people.

Run on the cement.

Hit each other.

Or,

Steal the balls from one another."

There I stood next to the line of cherubic little ones, and all I could think about was throwing sand, pushing people, running on the cement, hitting, and stealing balls from one another. I wondered if I as an adult have all those devious possibilities in mind, how much more so must these four year olds with immature brains? If I were them, I might just go ahead and throw sand. Of course, I understand each person is responsible for their own actions, but I bet it would help if we avoided planting these ideas in their heads in the first place. She was well meaning, but she was sending the wrong message. Planting the wrong script. When we plant wrong scripts like this one, we'd better be ready to reap a negative crop.

What if she had taken a more positive approach? So often as a mom I get caught up in all the "do nots" instead of the "dos" of teaching and training my kids. I forget how very much I encourage them with my positive reinforcement and belief in them to do their best. Let's be realistic. *They are kids.* They are sinful at heart just like you and me. They will have bad days and certain issues that need careful attention and prayer. But for the most part, we can do a lot of good for our children by believing the best of them, speaking about the actions and attitudes *we want to see* more than *what we don't want to see*, and breathing life into their hearts.

I Thessalonians 5:11 says, "Therefore encourage one another and build one another up, just as you are doing." Are my instructions meant to "build one another up" or only to give orders? It's beautiful to think that in the simple things of parenting, like teaching my kids to clean their room, that something so mundane could actually be something holy. My parenting transcends from managing the avalanche of needs to riding the waves of opportunity toward Christ-likeness. Parents are given the great responsibility to minister to their children, instilling in them a desire to seek God and find Him. If we are continually nagging them, pointing out their faults, and telling them what not to do, we tear them down instead of building them up. Their hearts become as steely as the robots we fashion them into by our barking orders and rude demands.

Instead of gruff commands, I have learned to speak lovingly and truthfully to my children. Colossians 4:6 says, "Let your speech always be gracious, seasoned with salt, so that you may know how you ought to answer each person." One way I do that is by incorporating Scripture into my instructions. In our book, *Triggers*, Wendy reminds us to use Scripture like a scalpel and not a hammer, but organically weaving the Word of God into our parenting scripts transforms both us and our kids. After all, **God writes every righteous script**. And then He places us on stage in our living rooms to live it out. As we progress through this book, you will notice the parenting scripts we use with our own kids are rooted in biblical truths.

God writes every righteous script.

PARENTING SCRIPT:

Reversing my defensive language and motivating my boys with a gentle and positive approach takes place in the every-day activities we encounter as a family. Whenever we get in the car, I take a few minutes to pray aloud with my boys. It usually sounds something like this:

> *"Dear Father, thank You for our wonderful and comfortable car that we get to drive in. Please keep Your protection around us as we drive. Thank You for Oliver who I know is going to have a kind spirit toward every child in his classroom today, and thank You that Oliver listens and obeys. Thank You for Quinn who I know has a sharing heart and who will give to others. I'm sure he will let others go first today. Thank You for Oakley who says kind words to his brother, like 'You are a good basketball player.' And thank You for this day that You have made for us to be an example to others. In Jesus' name we pray, amen!"*

A quick glance in the rearview mirror and all three have happy little smiles on their faces, *ready to prove me right*. I remember one of the first times I saw the power of positive reinforcement when Quinn was four years old. I went to pick him up from his preschool class. His teacher came right up to me to tell me that he was an exceptional sharer that day and that he was given a special sticker for his kindness to the other kids. Wouldn't you know it? We had prayed and talked specifically about sharing on the drive to class. This is true of all my boys, time and time again. On the days we talk about helping the teacher and asking if there is anything they can do to serve their peers, the teachers tell me what amazing helpers they were that day. The days we discuss how we can give sincere encouragement with our words to our friends, their teachers tell me what nice things my kids said to others.

As kids mature, the positive script changes to fit their age and stage of life:

"I noticed you have a lot of homework from your classes lately, Justin. It'd be amazing to see you organizing your schedule in the afternoons to make sure it's being completed on time. If you find an organizer or app you like, I'll buy it for you. I'll even throw in extra snacks and sports drinks for you to share with your buddies after school the more I see you being responsible. You are going to be the most popular middle school study partner around."

"When we go into the store today, let's be happy for Oakley who is spending his allowance money on a toy for himself. I'd love to hear each of you give him a word of encouragement to honor the patience he displayed to save his money for this special occasion. Who wants to go first?"

"Quinn, it's so nice to see that you always put your shoes in the basket by the front door. I bet you can do that with your backpack too by hanging it on the coat rack. In fact, I'm going to be watching to see what a great job you do for the next week!"

"Oliver, I know it can be hard being the oldest of four brothers, but I'm so thankful God made you a leader. I like hearing you pray for your friends at bedtime. It's a wonderful example to them. Keep it up!"

"Sarah, you are earning my trust more and more now that you are a teen. I love being able to give you freedom. If you keep going in this direction, I bet you will earn the privilege to drive my car to school. In fact, if you would like to wash the car the next two Saturdays without me asking you again, I'll know I can really trust you to take care of my car when I'm not around. I'm excited for you."

I'm not interested in getting kudos as a mom or micro-managing my kids into having good behavior for the sake of outward appearances. Our conversations always involve the reason why we do this—to be an example of how Christ loves us, to obey His Word, and to be a light to others that we may honor and love God and people. Remember, God writes every righteous script—His Scriptures that we can weave into our parenting. There is a time and a place to tell kids not to throw sand. Certainly it's important to set rules for safety and everyone's well-being. But I am convinced that we often undermine ourselves with our script of "dont's" instead of modeling and expressing the "dos."

Try it for a while. Put on a Philippians 4:8 mentality toward your kids and even your spouse:

"Finally, brothers and sisters, whatever is true, whatever is noble, whatever is right, whatever is pure, whatever is lovely, whatever is admirable—if anything is excellent or praisewor-thy—think about such things."

Talk with them about the fruit of the Spirit you want to see from their hearts and equip them with the Truth to live it out. Be their biggest cheerleader, advocate, prayer warrior, and model. Line 'em up and straighten 'em out. But please, let's fill the minds of our children with nobility, purity, and whatever is praiseworthy as they head out our doors. Before we know it they will be leaving our homes as adults into the world at large. Plant a seed of trust and water it with words of admiration while they are young, and I dare say that when they are grown, they will flourish into what we believed they were all along. And they won't just be good citizens, they will be lights on a hill because they learned how to shine on the playground.

SCRIPT-URE:

"Therefore encourage one another and build one another up, just as you are doing"

(I Thessalonians 5:11)

PRAYER SCRIPT:

Dear Lord, I have felt like parenting is more of a burden than a joy, and my negative approach is doing more harm than good. I confess that I often want to control my kids and my circumstances instead of enjoying them. However, what I really want to be is a mom/dad who builds up my kids and does not simply boss them around. Help me to know what to say and when to say it to meet the needs of my child as an individual. Give me eyes to see the best in my children as gifts God has given to me! May my kids feel my pleasure in being their parent at all times, even when I am teaching and training them. In Jesus' name, amen!

MAKE THE SCRIPT YOUR OWN:

How would you describe your approach to motivating your kids to do what you want them to do? Is your parenting in general more of a negative approach or a positive one? Do you consider your role as a parent an opportunity to build up and encourage your kids? Think of a common scenario in your home when your script is less than positive. In the workbook pages, write out your own script for when your child needs positive reinforcement that fits your own family dynamics.

Chapter 3 —
During Naptime and
Dinnertime Struggles

Wendy

I recently stopped by a young mom's house to drop off a meal. She'd just given birth to her third child and needed more than just a casserole, so I sent my teenager out into the back yard to watch her two toddlers play. After putting the tupperware in the fridge, I set to work on her sink full of dirty dishes. As I washed, she nursed the baby at the kitchen table, and we talked.

We transitioned naturally from fun stories about the baby to a heavier conversation about the two older kids. Hormones and sleeplessness intensified my friend's emotions, and as she nursed and shared, she cried. The one straw that seemed to break her back more consistently than all the others each afternoon was naptime. I nodded, remembering. A tough naptime struggle every now and again is hard, but when the struggle over naps becomes a daily habit it can be exhausting!

"It's like we've gotten into a bad habit somehow with them not napping and me acting like a raving lunatic each afternoon!" She laughed awkwardly and then continued, "Sometimes I spank them, I almost always threaten them, other times I use a bribe … on the days the baby is already asleep I just crawl into bed with the big kids and we all fall asleep. I want to be consistent and calm, I just don't know how. So I start doing whatever comes to my mind."

We all know how important consistency is in parenting. We've read it in just about every parenting book we've ever picked up—even the one we read in the OB GYN's office during our very first pregnancy. Consistency is key! We get it! **But what's a mom or dad to do when the only thing they're consistent at is being inconsistent?** My sweet friend was so insightful to point out how she tries a different thing every day in her attempt to get her young children, still in need of naps, to obey.

But what's a mom or dad to do when the only thing they're consistent at is being inconsistent?

I put down the dishtowel and took the baby from her arms, giving the newborn some gentle pats on her back until she let out a little burp. When I sat down at the table I said, "Inconsistency is simply a bad habit, but consistency is a habit too. What's more, it's a habit you can get yourself and your children into, but you've got to make a plan. You've got to plan your habits."

She started to cry again and I reached over the baby and touched her arm, "No …" I soothed, "this is good news. You don't have to keep doing the same thing. You get to make a change and bring your children with you. Make a plan with your husband tonight. Ask him for his perspective and come up with a plan."

When my big kid came inside with his two young charges, we said goodbye and drove home. As we drove, I remembered naptimes in our home a decade ago. The big kid beside me in the passenger seat was my most excellent napper! He napped all the way through his kindergarten year. His middle brother, however, decided to give up napping at two.

I was the queen of inconsistency with my sweet little exhausted (and exhausting) lamb. Like my young friend, sometimes I threatened, other times I bribed, and often I simply fell asleep with him in the last minutes of my oldest child's naptime. That is, until I made a different plan.

I'm always cautious about sharing parenting scripts because Amber and I don't believe in one-size-fits-all answers. We want each response to be Holy Spirit-inspired for your own unique little family, not formulaic. As a matter of fact, the two of us often write ourselves completely different parenting scripts. She's known to nap with her toddler, while I transition my kids from naptime to quiet time in their beds and bedrooms alone.

What's the right plan for one family isn't necessarily the best plan for another. The trick is consistency. However, let this relieve some stress—you're allowed to make a plan that ends up being the wrong plan, and you're allowed to make a new plan. Just don't try something new each and every day. Make a plan and give it a go for the next few months. If it doesn't fit, write yourself a new script.

PARENTING SCRIPT:

Back in those early days when my middle boy refused to sleep, I made a plan. Because he was so young, there didn't need to be much talk, just a simple routine. First, I'd tuck his older brother into bed, turn off his bedroom light, pull the blinds down, then I'd sing a song and close the door. Next, I'd return to my youngest child's room to read a couple of books in his rocking chair and sing a special little song that was just ours. And then, every afternoon I'd say the exact same words, "Sweet Brody, it's time for some quiet time in your bed. You can sleep if you're tired, or play with your stuffed animals, or read your books. I know you can stay in your room quietly, because big brother's sleeping. I'll be back after your quiet time."

It all sounds much too perfect when I write the script this way, however, truth be told, my baby boy fought me tooth and nail for a long time. But I remained consistent. And when I gave birth to my third son, I kept at it with Brody because I needed that quiet hour each day as much as he did.

Go ahead, practice this script with me: "Sweet _____, it's time for some quiet time in your bed. You can sleep if you're tired, or play with your stuffed animals, or read your books. Stay in your room, because our family is all resting. I'll be back after your quiet time."

Be consistent and eventually you'll find yourself in a new routine with a new habit. Of course this isn't just about naptimes, but anytime you've gotten yourself into an inconsistent habit. Dinnertime for instance can be a miserable time of the day, so make a plan and then stick to it. Simply let your yes mean yes, let your no mean no, let your naptime mean naptime, and let your "three bites of veggies before you get a cookie" mean "three bites of veggies before you get a cookie." If they refuse to sleep, you can choose to let them be exhausted, but *you don't have to be.* At the end of their "quiet time" (and I use that term loosely), go to them with a sincere smile, kiss their sweaty little upturned face and tousle their curls, and greet them with a smile and a song. Let your yes be yes ...

"But above all, my brethren, do not swear, either by heaven or by earth or with any other oath; but your yes is to be yes, and your no, no, so that you may not fall under judgment" (James 5:12, NASB).

Because of our work with moms and dads who struggle with anger, we've heard hundreds of tearful confessions. Parents, in their exasperation, don't only swear by heaven, they swear directly at their young kids—cursing their children over naptime struggles and at the dinner table too. I choose to believe parents want to act gently, with the authority that their yes can simply be yes and their no, no. Unfortunately, when children don't obey, parents tend to forget their own authority and start floundering. Floundering equals inconsistency, and inconsistency only undermines one's authority further and leads to more bad family habits.

As the child of a very consistent and unchanging God, I know from experience that God's unwavering character and promises won't ever change. His consistency brings me peace in the steadfast knowledge that He is trustworthy. Our kids need to know this about us too. They can trust that when we say they can have cookie after they eat their veggies, they can have a cookie after they eat their veggies. But when we say that they won't get a cookie if they've cried for twenty minutes straight after throwing their broccoli on the floor, then they won't have that cookie. **Often, in my desire to teach them grace and give them second chances, I set us all up for a long childhood of whining voices, asking, "Can I earn the cookie back?"**

"No." Simply and lovingly, no. "But you can have one tomorrow night after you eat your dinner without throwing a fit. You can trust me, sweetheart. When you obey at dinnertime, there's a cookie. When you throw a fit, no cookie. I'm not going to change my mind. You can trust me ... I've got a plan." Hebrews 13:8 shows us what consistency looks like: "Jesus Christ is the same yesterday and today and forever." Let Him be your example as you parent consistently.

SCRIPT-URE:

"But above all, my brethren, do not swear, either by heaven or by earth or with any other oath; but your yes is to be yes, and your no, no, so that you may not fall under judgment"

(James 5:12, NASB)

PRAYER SCRIPT:

Dear Lord, thank you for singing over us with joyful songs. You are strong and mighty and trustworthy and consistently good. You don't change. Help us, Lord, to parent our children as You parent us. Give us a sense of our authority in You, so that when our children push against us, we don't become inconsistent or give into anger and falter. We need Your Spirit to inspire us with the right words, the right plan, to form the right and righteous habits for our specific family in our specific home. Yes, we need Your help, Holy Spirit. Give us wisdom, we pray in Jesus' name, amen.

MAKE THE SCRIPT YOUR OWN:

Consider what habits you would like to put into place. Whether around the dinner table at night or during afternoon naps, make a plan. As you do, remember to give yourself some margin for the days you're running home late from preschool or a last minute invite to a friend's house. Be careful to know the difference between consistency and legalism. **Consistency always leaves room for grace ...** and plenty of cuddles. In the workbook pages, write out a dinner routine or a tuck-in ritual (perhaps with a gently lullaby script) that fits your family best.

Consistency always leaves room for grace ...

Chapter 4 — When Your Child Is Irresponsible

Amber

Kate thought she was being a loving mom.

"Dear Amber," she wrote ...

> I need some insight into a situation I am having with my teenage son, Thomas. I try to wake him up on time for breakfast so I can take him to carpool, but he is always late. I leave him at home, drop off the other kids, and drive back home to get him so he doesn't miss his classes. He just doesn't seem to care or listen to me! What can I do to motivate him? I'm afraid he is going to get a suspension if he is late again.

I just about choked on my own morning oatmeal when I read this reader's letter. Kate's heart was in the right place, but her good intentions were sabotaging her son's maturity and ability to grow into an adult with a healthy understanding of natural consequences. Natural consequences may go against our nature as parents, but they allow kids to take ownership for their choices and feel the weight of their responsibilities.

Here's what I wrote back to Kate:

"The best thing you can do for Thomas is to let him fail. Failure teaches us what works and what doesn't—a vital life lesson."

Here's a PARENTING SCRIPT for this situation:

Thomas, I love you. Because I love you, a hot breakfast will be ready for you every school day at 7:30. I will be leaving the house at 8:00 am to take the carpool kids to school, and when I return, I will not be able to make a second trip back to the school anymore because it is a problem for me. If you would like to get to class on time, then I have every belief in you that you can be in the car at 8:00 am.

I went on to share a little more advice with Kate:

> Then, stick to it. Let him fail. Let him get suspended! Talk with your school's staff or his teacher, so it is a team effort. Being a helicopter parent who hovers over your child and swoops in to rescue him from every challenge will only serve to undermine him later in life. As a teen, the stakes are low. A suspension isn't great, but it's far better to be kicked out of school for a few days than to get fired from his dream job after college because he never learned to get somewhere on time. The stakes when he is an adult are high. Better to let him experience the natural consequences from the school now, than to let him flounder when he is grown up.

> If he gets upset or protests, simply show him sincere empathy. Say something like, "I know it's a bummer that you are suspended. But, Honey, I believe in you! I

know you can do better next time!" Place the responsibility back where it belongs: on Thomas.

Parents, this same principle applies to even younger kids too. I have taken my kids to school in their pajamas, and they have shown up without shoes at church more than once. Again, the key is to talk with the teacher first to come to some agreeable terms that work for all of you, but be creative and tailor this concept to your particular situation. Sure, they protest at being ushered to the car in that state, but you and I can still remain calm, empathetic, and consistent.

Allowing our children to fail because they are making poor choices also creates humility. They realize that the burden is theirs alone to either remove or endure. In the same way, whether we are hesitant to let our kids play football or study abroad, letting them be brave—even letting them falter—creates character.

The Bible puts it like this:

"More than that, we rejoice in our sufferings, knowing that suffering produces endurance, and endurance produces character, and character produces hope, and hope does not put us to shame, because God's love has been poured into our hearts through the Holy Spirit who has been given to us" (Romans 5:35).

"... The son shall not suffer for the iniquity of the father, nor the father suffer for the iniquity of the son. The righteousness of the righteous shall be upon himself, and the wickedness of the wicked shall be upon himself" (Ezekiel 18:20).

If failing or letting kids struggle to figure things out on their own is so good for them, why is it so hard for us as parents to allow that in their lives? There are several reasons:

1. Love

   Because we love our sons and daughters, we confuse shel-
   tering them from pain or suffering with caring for them.
   Thus, we delay important life lessons they should learn as
   we nudge them from the nest.

2. Embarrassment

   We are embarrassed by what others may think if our child
   fails or makes wrong choices. I often like to say, "Never
   make choices because of your fears or peers!" Don't worry
   about what others think. This is *your* child and those who
   are on your side wouldn't judge you anyway.

3. Fear

   There's that fear word again. It's easy to let our imagina-
   tions run away with us and forecast the worst-case scenario if our kids fail—but don't let your mind play tricks
   on you. In most cases, the setbacks they experience aren't
   that important in the grand scheme of life; but even if they
   are, ultimately, it is their responsibility and they need to
   take ownership. You simply can't do that for them.

4. Habit

   When our kids are newborns, they are entirely dependent
   on us for survival. As they develop, we see their rapid
   growth, but we don't pace with them in our parenting. We
   have to relinquish the habit of micro-
   managing them and study what is
   developmentally age appropriate so
   we don't stifle them!

   Allowing kids to experience natural consequences and appropriate failure does not ruin them. It rescues them from an indecisive and entitled future.

   Believe the best about your children
   and be their biggest cheerleader. A
   positive attitude goes a long way
   in convincing kids to do their best!
   Ultimately, they will choose their
   own path and we need to let them.

Allowing kids to experience natural consequences and appropriate failure does not ruin them. It rescues them from an indecisive and entitled future.

SCRIPT-URE:

"More than that, we rejoice in our sufferings, knowing that suffering produces endurance, and endurance produces character, and character produces hope, and hope does not put us to shame, because God's love has been poured into our hearts through the Holy Spirit who has been given to us"

Romans 5:35.

PRAYER SCRIPT:

"Dear Lord, it's hard to see my children make bad choices. My heart hurts for them. I want to rescue them, but I know that is not always the best way for them to learn their lessons. Help me to communicate my expectations clearly and allow my children to make their own choices. When they fail, help them to learn from their mistakes, Lord. Thank You for loving us too much to allow us to go down a wrong path without Your loving correction. I trust You are with my child, even when they bring suffering upon themselves. Help me to be empathetic in those moments of need. Thank You, Lord! In Jesus' name, amen!

MAKE THE SCRIPT YOUR OWN:

In what areas does your child show irresponsibility? How can you allow him or her to feel the weight of responsibility without taking it upon yourself? Is there some modeling or coaching that you need to do first in order to clearly communicate expectations? What prevents you from doing so? Write out your own script for when your child is irresponsible that fits your own family dynamics.

Chapter 5 —
When Children
Ignore Authority

Wendy

It was a simple exchange between grandma and grandson. The eight-year-old boy asked the seventy-two-year-old lady if he could have a piece of gum from her purse, and the answer came back "No, not now." By the way, this particular grandma loves to say yes all day long. On this particular day, she'd been making "deposits" of affirmation into his little love tank. "Yes, I'll fry up some bacon for breakfast. Yes, I'll watch you build Legos. Yes, we can make a batch of cookies this after-noon. Yes …" But this one request was met with a simple no.

Only a few minutes later grandma found grandson chewing on a great big wad of Hubba Bubba that he'd snagged from a brother's bottom (treasure) drawer.

I had just come home from running errands and watched my son ignore his grandma's authority and sneak off to do whatever pleased him. I had a choice to make—how was I going to respond? And isn't that the truth about parenting? We have choices all day long. Choice after choice after good parenting choice about how to respond to our children. The problems start for us when we forget that we have choices about what we say and how we say it. And so I thought it all through as I unpacked the groceries. I asked the little culprit to take out the trash, and he gave me a big toothy grin with bright pink gum stuck to his lips. As I put the pasta, rice, and peanut butter in the pantry, he took out the trash. And as he took out the trash I considered my response.

A little while later, when grandma and the other two were onto their next bit of fun, I asked the little boy with the big will to join me in my room. When he came in I held out a piece of tissue and asked him to spit out his gum. The sparkle dimmed in his eyes, and he knew what was coming.

Our children don't need us to berate them with what they've done wrong. They know.

He said with a shrug, "It was all out of flavor anyway."

Deep breath.

Before launching into my predetermined script, I reminded myself that I didn't want to talk about gum, I wanted to talk about his heart, "For the Lord does not look at the things that people look at. People look at the outward appearance, but the Lord looks at the heart" (1 Samuel 16:7). Talking about one singular bad behavior at a time is like trying to get rid of a dandelion with a lawnmower. The issue wasn't the gum, as I saw it, the issue wasn't even my child's sneakiness, the issue was (and always is) sin. Heart sin. So my goal was to talk to him about his heart.

Come to think of it, I didn't even want to talk about his eight-year-old heart. My job, as I see it, is to cast a vision for his future heart! I desire for him to have a life of virtuous character, and a child who doesn't honor authority will likely grow into an adult who doesn't honor authority. That's the heart issue I was prepared to talk about.

"Hey dude," I started, "your grandma had so much fun watching you and your brothers play this morning. Don't you love it when she drives down to spend the weekend with us?"

Getting our little people nodding and smiling is good for the soil of their hearts! So often we want to go pound seeds into hard soil, but talking about positives first helps to turn and condition the soil, making hearts soft and receptive to fruit-bearing seeds.

"Speaking of your grandma, when I came in from the grocery store I heard you ask her for a piece of gum and she said no, but then you went and took one anyway."

Most kids will break into a defensive song and dance about why they did what they did, how it was justified, and how the whole of their juvenile life isn't fair! My child is no different, and justified his actions with the simple fact he didn't take *her* gum, he took someone else's. Here's what I said:

"Darling, I actually wasn't asking you why you did it or how you did it or if grandma was right to say no to you or not. I simply commented that you didn't respect her answer even though she was the one in charge. So, I've got a question for you. Are you ready?"

(Remember, mom and dad, there's no fight in you, this is merely a conversation you've planned out for times such as these.)

PARENTING SCRIPT:

"What are you going to do when your teacher says you can't use a pen on your paper, only a pencil. Are you going to do whatever you want, or will you respect her because she's in charge?"

"I'll respect her!" 99.9999% of kids will respond positively to this question.

"How about this one: When you're a grown man and your boss tells you you've got to stay late to finish a job, but you really want to go see a movie with some of your friends, will you stay and do what he asked or will you sneak off and do what you want?"

Your child may wrestle with this one a bit, but they will most likely concede to doing right.

"I believe that you will do what's right! I do. God did an awesome job when He made you with a heart that longs to do what's right and honor others, but you've got to grow that muscle of obedience, just like every other muscle in your body that you want to get big and strong."

When our children flex their muscular wills and do what's wrong, we can affirm their strength and encourage them to use their muscle to do right.

A few days after this conversation I pulled a stick of gum out, offered it to my boy and asked him to go out back with me for a game of HORSE. As we shot some hoops I told him this story.

"You know the band 21 Pilots?"

"Yeah," he said with a smile, after making a sweet swoosh. "They sing the song 'Stressed Out.'" I waited for him to sing through a verse and the chorus two times before going on.

"Well, did you know that the lead singer was homeschooled?"

"No," replied my kid.

"Yeah, he was. But before he started taking his music seriously he wanted desperately to be a professional basketball player." Again, swoosh. My child beamed because he loves basketball and is homeschooled and wants to one day be a professional musician. The seed I was purposefully planting was going down deep into fertile soil because the time was right. "So, the story goes that his mom told him that every single homeschool day he had to make five hundred baskets. They didn't have to be in a row, but he had to make five hundred baskets."

"No way! I couldn't make one hundred!" He exclaimed.

"Maybe, not at first anyway, but you could eventually. If you practiced. The point is, son, anything you really want to do right, you've got to exercise that muscle."

"Like practicing my guitar," he said with conviction.

"Like practicing your guitar, or shooting hoops, or even honoring your grandma when she says no to a piece of gum."

Swoosh.

SCRIPT-URE:

"He who restrains his words has knowledge, and he who has a cool spirit is a man of understanding"

(Proverbs 17:27)

PRAYER SCRIPT:

Dear Lord, You've always been slow to anger and abounding in lovingkindness with me. You've led me to repentance with your kindness, not your harsh and hustled responses. Help me to follow Your example and carefully choose words that honor

You. Give me a vision for the long-term goal as well. Not just right behavior, but right hearts; and not simply right hearts for today, but right hearts for the future, as they grow into men and women who love and honor You, Lord. Let them learn to honor You as I teach them to honor me. In Jesus' name and for His glory I pray, amen."

MAKE THE SCRIPT YOUR OWN:

It's okay to not respond to wrong behavior immediately. This is especially true if your knee-jerk reactions aren't the right ones. **Take your time, and figure out the right response before you react. Just because we don't parent in the problem doesn't mean we don't mother every moment.** Same is true for you dads … In our book, *Triggers*, Amber and I lay down the foundation for this book with these words: Figure out what you mean to say before you say something mean. If what you've been saying to your son or daughter when they've ignored your authority hasn't worked, take some time to plan a better response. In the workbook pages, come up with some new words to use with your child when they go their own way and willfully do their own thing.

Chapter 6 —
When Your Body
Language Is Your Script

Amber

She flipped her dark hair over her shoulder and stood up from the table. "Delightful to meet you," she said as she excused herself from the meeting. We had been collaborating for an advertising project, but during our time together she had tilted her chair away from me so I could only see her profile. The way she gathered her papers and quickly exited the room as if she didn't have the time of day for what I had to say spoke volumes. There I sat in my swivel chair across from several creative geniuses, discussing culture and making small talk. The temperature in the room warmed up as soon as she left. Nothing about her limp handshake and assurance that meeting me was "delightful" convinced me.

I could tell she felt quite the opposite about my place on her team. Her boss, Janet, had courted me for months to come on board, but she clearly didn't feel married to the relationship. "How exactly did she get this role?" she questioned her in front of me as if I wasn't even in the room. My read of her opinion became that much clearer weeks later when she ousted me from the project we were working on in favor of her replacement—a friend of hers. It stung at first, but I counted my blessings that I dodged a bullet. The project quickly went down in a blaze of fury, and I was thankful God spared me from being entrenched in something I would have regretted.

Body language betrays or bolsters verbal language. Our words are only a secondary part of communication. The way we say something and how we look when we say it are the real communicators. **Body language betrays or bolsters verbal language.** Most of us have probably experienced the impact of nonverbal communication in the workplace or in our friendships, but there is no place more important to realize how loudly our actions speak than in our homes.

When my fourth son, Quade, was born last year, I looked drunk on love, and I didn't mind a bit. I could literally feel my face muscles aching from smiling and doting on him. I beamed with joy over this unexpected gift of a son, and everyone could read it on my face. No words were necessary. When I did speak, I made no apologies for the sing-songy, high-pitched tone of my voice. I was just that darn happy about being his mom. I wish I could say I always had that kind of loving body language in every encounter with my kids. When my husband Guy and I were parenting three boys who were four-years-old and younger, there were just as many frowns and scowls as there were hands on hips and crossed arms. Eventually, we learned to retrain the way we communicate with our bodies. Less demonstrative disapproval and more expressive empathy and grace, which meant less pursed lips, rubbing of temples, and tense shoulders, and more relaxed faces, deep breaths, and tender eyes. Calm and self-controlled conversations replaced shrill reactions.

PARENTING SCRIPT:

Consider what script are we saying with our faces? Lips? Eyes? Hands? Shoulders? The script I desire to shout from the rooftops is found in a gentle face, a relaxed body, and an empathetic expression. My sons read it in the tender way I take their hands in the middle of a tearful gasping confession, and they take it in by my arm around their shoulder and my willingness to say, "Let's breathe together for a moment. Let me help you become calm so I can help you. Inhale with me for three seconds, and let's exhale for four. Come on, let's just breathe. I care."

My body-script penetrates their heart as I sincerely and lovingly tell them that though I think they have made a wrong choice, I know they can try again next time. My small smile conveys my sincerity. I tousle their hair as I tell them I'm going to say a quick prayer for them so that next time when they struggle, they become victorious over the temptation. My bowed head conveys my commitment to the Lord and my commitment to them.

Recently two of my kids were arguing over personal space on the family couch. Someone's toes got a little too close to someone else's leg. These are the itty bitty, silly struggles that make parents miserable. There are plenty of times I have rushed over to my kids with an incredulous, "Really guys? Are you really arguing over something so small? Can't you just …?" My voice is either exasperated and whiny myself, or short and angry. I've learned that joining in their immaturity this way does not model what I want to see in my kids. Instead I alter the tone of my voice to be as silly as their argument. "Whata ya doin?" I say in an exaggerated Italian accent. "Oakley-ah, you gotta be-ah kiddin me. His toes-ah are so-ah cute-ah!" The tension melts and two little boys begin to giggle. Just as my body language can elicit tears of shame or peals of laughter, my tone of voice can become a flamethrower or a merry-maker too. We spent the rest of the day channeling our inner Italian heritage, lightening the mood, and enjoying one another. I changed my menu to include pizza for dinner. May as well go all out!

Proverbs 17:22 says, "A joyful heart is good medicine, but a crushed spirit dries up the bones." And Matthew 15:18 says, "But the things that come out of a person's mouth come from the heart, and these defile them" (NIV). The root of every word we say and how we say it both in tone and body language reveals what is in our hearts. Joyful words are the echo of a merry heart, rooted in Christ-likeness. If we say we are Christ-followers but continually treat our children with insensitivity and speak to them rudely and with contempt, we are deceiving ourselves. We aren't deceiving our kids, however. They get the message loud and clear. God, in all His holiness and discernment, has given us a precious gift in the role of parenthood, and He will call us to account for how we steward His blessings to us. Do we treat them as bothersome objects of our disappointment and wrath, or do we look on them with love, even when they sin, and coach them toward right behavior with loving-kindness like Jesus does for us?

There are a handful of questions I ask myself when I know my communication is sending the wrong message:

What is really bothering me about this? Am I taking my own adult brand of issues out on my kids? Is it that they are interrupting my peace and quiet? Am I angry because they are acting immature, though age-appropriate, or because they are sinning against God? Have I done a long and intense time of spiritual training and practical modeling regarding this issue with my children so they know what is right and what my expectations are? If I were on the receiving end of this conversation, how would I feel as a child? Would I want anyone to talk to me this way? Is there a better way to get my point across right now? Would my child say that I have confronted them in love with the goal of restoring them relationally?

When we find we have treated our kids with contempt through our words, tone, or body language, we need to make the wrong right. It's humbling to go to our children and apologize, but it's that humility that begins the work of transforming us through the Holy Spirit so our fathering and mothering become more like the heavenly Father. If this is an ongoing issue for you, make it a habit to picture a mirror in front of your face when you are talking with your kids. If you don't like what you see, change it. Revisit the Scripture we prayed together in Chapter One: Let Psalm 51:1-2 become your prayer:

> *"Create in me a clean heart, O God, and renew a right spirit within me. Cast me not away from your presence, and take not your Holy Spirit from me. Restore to me the joy of your salvation, and uphold me with a willing spirit."*

If you are reading this book, your spirit is willing. There is hope for change for anyone who is seeking to do the right thing, no matter how much time has passed or the age of your kids. For some of us, becoming a new creation will take concentrated and purposeful action, one encounter with our kids at a time. Time will pass anyway. Use it to be a blessing in your home. Just as right words are the overflow of a right heart, let your posture be the product of your godly purpose as a parent.

One day, when our sons and daughters are grown, they will look at pictures of us and the images they view on photo paper will not be the only ones they see. Their mind's eye will give them the most accurate picture of who we were. If we yield to God's help, they will remember the way we stood before them with wide and welcoming arms. They will recall our firm but tender words. And the script they will hear will not be one that conveys disapproval and condemnation but one of joy that reflected our hearts and the privilege it was to be their parents.

SCRIPT-URE:

"Create in me a clean heart, O God, and renew a right spirit within me. Cast me not away from your presence, and take not your Holy Spirit from me. Restore to me the joy of your salvation, and uphold me with a willing spirit"

(Psalm 51:1-12)

PRAYER SCRIPT:

Lord, I know I'm communicating the wrong message with my tone of voice and my body language. Please make me mindful, so I don't react to my kids' behavior with aggravation. Help my first response to be one that seeks to understand and listen. Give me a tongue that speaks the truth in love. Allow my physical response to communicate loving kindness. From my face to my feet, Lord, let me convey my care for them. Father, thank You for never leaving me on my own in my parenting or keeping a record of my wrongs. Let me love my kids with that same kind of unconditional love. Let them always remember me as a mom or dad who welcomed them, even in their sinful moments, into my grace and mercy. In Jesus' name, amen!

MAKE THE SCRIPT YOUR OWN:

What happens to your body when you become angry or frustrated by your child's behavior? What tone of voice is most often the one your kids hear? How is this different than what you desire to communicate to them? In the workbook pages, write out a body language script that fits your own family dynamics.

Chapter 7 —
When Siblings Fight

Wendy

There are mornings I wake up to the peaceful sound of birds chirping, but more often than not I come to consciousness with the soundtrack of fighting cranked up down the hall.

Our home has lacked peace in recent days. It seems not thirty seconds pass without injustice or insults flying between siblings. And yes, if you're wondering, it is exhausting. However, it's not just exhausting for me. I can see on their faces that my kids are worn out by it too. They're caught in a negative pattern together, tearing each other down.

My tendency, I confess, is to jump into the metaphorical boxing ring with them and join the fight. **Trouble is, our fighting with them doesn't teach them not to fight. Perhaps you've tried to fight the fight out of your kids too.** So we have a choice to make: either jump into the ring and start swinging, or walk around the outside of the ropes and call your kids back to their corners.

DING DING DING "Everyone to your corners!"

Gently, with tender tones, we can lean over the ropes, whisper into velvet soft ears, and remind them (yet again) how it is we love one another in our house. "Hey son, I'm not going to fight with you. I'll fight for you, but not with you."

Write Romans 12:21 on post-it notes and stick them all around your house, and write it on your heart as well, "Do not be overcome by evil but overcome evil with good." **Moms and dads, don't join the fight. You'll never win the war that way.** The only sure way to beat your children's evil is by overcoming it with good. So climb out of the ring if you're already engaged in the fight, and move yourself around to their corner. Take off your gloves and say, "Nope, I won't fight with you. I'm here to love you and teach you, but I'm not here to fight with you." Then drop the towel down on the mat between your children, and call the match off.

Moms and dads, don't join the fight. You'll never win the war that way.

DING DING DING "Everyone to your corners!"

PARENTING SCRIPT:

While this chapter may be lecture-long, the actual script is short and sweet. Because I'm prone to drone on and on at my kids, I've got to keep it simple—that way I'll remember to say it, and they'll remember to hear it. "Alright you guys, it doesn't matter who did wrong, or what happened—everybody to your rooms. Don't think of it as punishment or timeout. You're simply showing me you need some time away from one another."

DING DING DING "Everyone to your corners!"

Last night at the dinner table, in a rare moment of calm, I talked with the boys about their most recent fight.

"Boys, I want your eyes on me, because I'm going to tell you something that could change your life for the better. Not just here and now but better forever. Do you want that? Do you want things to be better here in our home? Do you want to have better relationships with one another and better relationships with all of the friends you're ever going to have?"

Of course they nodded.

As an aside: Let me take a moment to point out yet again I didn't bring up the specifics of their most recent wrong. They didn't need the reminder of who started it or what was said. They knew. There was no need to hash it all out again. And so it was, there at our family table, in a moment void of conflict, that I addressed the problem when we weren't having a problem. A couple of chapters back I advised: don't parent in the problem. Save the lesson for later. When all the angst has fizzled out, bring it up in such a way that gives them tools to do it better next time.

There at the dinner table I continued to speak out what I had already written down, my script. "You guys," I said, "God gave us one another, just the five of us around this table, to learn together how to treat people. If you can figure it out here, all of the relationships you'll ever have will go better!"

One child burst into a loud complaint about his brother, telling us all why being nice was going to be impossible because of him. I stayed calm and put my hand upon his arm, and waited for him to stop his tirade. "This is not a conversation." I was gentle but firm. "Please do not interrupt me again. Right now, I'm the only one talking."

The children around the table grew still. Because I wasn't fighting, they had no one to fight with. I continued in the stillness, "I'm going to tell you three things that will happen if you continue to argue with one another. Are you ready?" All eyes were on me.

THREE THINGS HAPPEN WHEN SIBLINGS ARGUE

1. "If you continue to yell at each other each day, you will damage your friendship. Not only will you be angry at each other today, but you will likely grow up to be angry at one another always." A couple of crocodile sized tears slipped down the plump cheeks of my youngest son. The other two shifted, convicted.

2. "On the flip side, if you learn to prefer your brothers, to encourage them and enjoy them, it will not only affect your friendship with them today, but it will set the stage for your friendship forever. And it can affect all of your other relationships beyond our family in the future. You will know how to honor and enjoy your friends, your college roommate and professors, your future boss and co-workers, your future neighbors, your wife, and even your own kids one day. Because you learned to enjoy your siblings, others will enjoy you! But if you choose to struggle as children, you will likely struggle with this as adults."

My husband let out a low moan in agreement and nodded with caring eyes. The children looked from their father to one another and then back to me. "Guys, this is where we learn it! God did such a good job when He gave us one another. Let's learn how to have good relationships where we encourage each other and build each other up."

I didn't even need to hit them over their heads with Scripture references because they'd hidden so many in their hearts already. Out they flowed.

"Mom, remember the verse, 'Encourage one another and build each other up'?"

"Exactly," I affirmed.

Another child chimed in, "How about 'Honor your father and your mother as the Lord your God has commanded you, so that all of your days will go great'!" I smiled at his translation and gave him a thumbs up across the dinner table.

"Boys, if we learn to honor one another right here in our home, God says our future and that also means our future friendships will go well. Who wants that?"

They all smiled at one another. Then the middle child asked, "What's number three? You said three things happen when we argue."

3. "Boys, this last one is just another sad side effect of what happens when you continue to argue with one another all day long: your father and I don't enjoy being around you. I know it sounds mean, but I also know this will make sense to you. It's not fun, and it doesn't feel good to have to constantly be breaking up fights. I'd rather bake cookies, laugh at your jokes, and watch funny videos with you on the ipad. When you fill our home with nasty arguments, your dad and I want to send you to your rooms or hide in ours."

"I don't want to argue anymore," said that middle boy. The other two looked at him lovingly in agreement.

Me too.

Me too.

Me too.

"One last thing, boys. I'm not going to give you warnings or reminders anymore. On the days you guys are struggling, I'm simply going to send you each to your rooms. You can play or read or listen to music by yourself, but you can't be together for one whole hour. I won't be angry at you, but I will do this each and every time so you can remember this important lesson.

SCRIPT-URE:

"Do not be overcome by evil but overcome evil with good"
(Romans 12:21)

PRAYER SCRIPT:

Dear Lord, Help me to be quick to listen to You and slow to speak to them. You know my tendency to fight when the kids fight. Their arguing makes me want to argue back. Help me, Holy Spirit, to slow down and consider what You would have me say. I pray a blessing over my children and their relationships with one another. I ask You, Lord, to teach them how to live peacefully here in our home, so they might live in peace with others once they are grown and gone. In Jesus' name I ask these things. Amen."

MAKE THE SCRIPT YOUR OWN:

I gave you a short script and a long one. Both are intended to inspire you to plan gentle words of your own when you are tempted to join the fight. In the heat of the battle, it's near impossible to come up with the right response. DING DING DING - send them to their corners. **Don't give in to the pressure to parent in the problem—address the problem when they aren't having one.** In the workbook pages, in this moment, before you run off to break up another fight, consider what you're going to say the next time the kids start fighting with one another again.

Chapter 8 —
When Your Child
Argues and Talks Back

Amber

The engine was barely off when my boys flung open the doors of the car and raced inside, straight for their electronic devices. The rule at our house is that they get thirty minutes on video games after school on Mondays, which they eagerly anticipate after a long workday in the classroom. But on this particular afternoon, I wanted them to help me unload groceries first.

"Boys! Put the ipads down—I want you to help me in the kitchen for a few minutes!" I called from down the hall.

Silence. Their eyes were fixated on the flashing lights and fast action on the screen. I made my way into the living room and put my hands on their shoulders to try again, "Gentlemen, I asked you to come and help me for a few minutes. Please pause your game and come to the kitchen."

"But Mom!" they shrieked! "*We haven't had our time yet!*"

Before I could respond, angry tears sprung to their eyes. I knew I was fighting a losing battle. I didn't want to argue with them. I simply wanted them to comply. I am the mom, and it seemed reasonable for me to get their help. They knew better than to protest too strongly, so they begrudgingly rose from the abyss of the couch and trudged to the kitchen to restock the cupboards.

Later that night my son said something that gave me pause for thought. "Mom" he said gently. "When you told us to help you in the kitchen today, it didn't feel fair. You promised us game time right after school, and you didn't keep your word. I'm sorry I reacted the way I did, but I wanted you to know."

You know what? *He was right!* I could have handled the situation much better. I should have kept in mind that they are kids who won't handle disappointment with the kind of maturity I was expecting. I didn't warn them in the car that I needed their help, nor did I respect them by allowing them the time I had already committed to giving them on their devices. While I didn't lose my cool, I was provoking them. Colossians 3:21 puts it like this: "Fathers, do not aggravate your children, or they will become discouraged" (NLT). Should my kids obey me when I ask them to do something, even in a moment like that? Yes. Was their reaction wrong? Yes. But mom messed up too. I was exercising my authority in a way that was bossy and disrespectful. I don't want my kids to obey just because I said so. I want them to obey from a place of affection.

After that night, I realized my kids desired to have a voice, but it was my place to teach them to resolve conflicts in a godly way. Their pattern of arguing over my requests wasn't working for anyone, and we needed a method to help us all communicate better. Proverbs 15:22 says, "Plans fail when there is no counsel, but with abundant advisers they are established." Together, we needed to devise a plan that allowed us to communicate in healthy ways instead of winging it and then reacting sinfully to one another.

When our kids feel powerless, their words sting, but when they feel heard, their voices are calm. I needed to coach them in speaking to me with respect, even if they disagree with me, and I needed to practice listening to them when they were willing to have an agreeable conversation about my decisions.

My husband and I decided to have a short family meeting where we explained that, from this point forward—when we make a decision as the parents, that they have a "right to appeal." I first heard this phrase from pastor Chuck Booher at Crossroads Christian Church here in California, and I love the message it communicates. Whenever the boys feel like my husband or I don't have enough information about an issue, or they feel we aren't being fair toward them, they can reason with us in a respectful tone and we will hear them out. We emphasize Proverbs 29:11 with them, "A fool vents all his feelings, but a wise man holds them back." There is a right way and a wrong way to express themselves!

My husband, Guy, and I make mistakes, and we want our kids to always feel like they can talk with us about issues. If my kids want to, they can even approach dad when I make a decision and ask for his help to approach me for appeal and vice versa. This process opens up pathways for healthy communication and takes away much of the angst and arguing because our kids know they can get further with us by speaking calmly and with respect than by arguing or yelling. Once we hear them out, our decision may change, or it may remain the same. Our final decision is just that— final. We expect them to honor our request.

PARENTING SCRIPT FOR THE RIGHT TO APPEAL:

Our afternoon scenario could have sounded like this:

Me: "Boys, pause your games and come to the kitchen to help me unload groceries!"

Son: "Mom, before we come to help you, may I appeal to you, please?"

Me: "Yes, you may. What would you like to say?"

Son: "You promised us we could have our electronics time right after school today. We have been really looking forward to it. I'm right in the middle of a hard level. If you let us finish, can we help you afterwards instead? And maybe even help you put the trash out?"

Me: "You know what Oliver? You are right. I did promise you your time and your request is reasonable. I understand what you are saying. Thanks for offering to also help with the trash. Go ahead and finish your game time and then come on into the kitchen. Thank you for speaking to me with respect. I love you!"

If I decide to stick with my first request, the Parenting Script would sound like this:

"Son, I appreciate the way you spoke to me and I hear you, but I'm going to stick with my first decision this time because I think it is best." My child's response then needs to be, "Okay, Mommy." And we leave it at that.

This kind of communication takes intentionality and time to practice with our kids. When we first introduced this concept, each day we took a few minutes to give our kids a scenario and asked them how they could handle it using the "right of appeal" and what they would say. We made the activity into a game, and made it fun! We also emphasized why this is a good way to communicate and we let them know that we value their insights and voices. We want to hear what is on their hearts! This made them feel secure, loved, and in control—all ingredients for more contented kids who are less prone to argue and push back in sinful ways. This process takes time for them to practice, but as we teach them and model what we want to see, this new habit forms. It's not going to look perfect every time, but giving them a right to appeal has relieved many of the tense moments of conflict that we used to endure on a regular basis.

Giving our kids some control doesn't mean we lose ours. It simply means they get to learn to experience control in a healthy way. How wonderful to toss them the keys and let them take their own personal power for a spin around the block while still under our watchful eye. The goal, of course, is to raise well-adjusted men and women who love God and others well, who know how to speak with respect and make good choices. If we are more interested in how well they obey us, even when they disagree with us, than learning to communicate respectfully, we may miss out on a wonderfully teachable moment.

Giving our kids some control doesn't mean we lose ours.

Let's empower our kids to think critically and speak logically rather than being ruled by emotions. Teaching them to talk with us removes the need for them to talk back to us.

And that's quite appealing indeed.

SCRIPT-URE:

"A fool vents all his feelings, but a wise man holds them back"
(Proverbs 29:11)

PRAYER SCRIPT:

Father, I can come to you at any time about anything and You hear me, even if I'm rough and raw with my words. I'm comforted that I can appeal to You and Your goodness. Help me to always be reasonable with my children. Help me to even be lavish in my willingness to hear their hearts like You are generous toward me when I cry out to You. Make my parenting heart more like Yours, Lord! And Father, help our family to grow in respect for one another. Allow us to use our tongues to honor and bless one another in increasing measure day by day. Help me as a parent to teach my children to communicate in appropriate ways and bless our home with peace. In Jesus' name, amen!

MAKE THE SCRIPT YOUR OWN:

Practice makes perfect! Think of a recent exchange with your child. Would having a "right to appeal" have made a difference? Put yourself in your child's shoes—would you want to have a voice in certain situations? These new ideas take time to foster, but they are worth it! What can you do to begin this process yourself, and how can you remember to persevere and not give up when the going gets rough? In the workbook pages, write out your own script for a right to appeal that fits your own family dynamics.

Chapter 9 — When They Cry Over Everything

Wendy

Babies cry. We expect them to. They communicate their needs through tears before they have words to tell us when they are hungry, tired, or in need of a fresh diaper. And we respond to their cries naturally and without angst.

I recall waking up, halfway down the hall, moving toward my infant in the middle of the night, still asleep but responding instinctively to his newborn cries. It was an unconscious sort of thing—before I was even awake I was coming to his aid.

There were times, however, when all the loving comfort in the world wouldn't (couldn't) quiet him down. Not knowing what to say or what to do, I asked a friend for help, and she taught me the fine art of baby swaddling. At first I thought it was crazy to mummify my tiny child and shush repeatedly into his small, sweet ear, but she assured me that tightly swaddling and shushing my crying baby may just work.

It did!

He began sleeping for longer periods and crying less. Settling him back down into his crib one night it suddenly made sense to me: swaddling an agitated baby recreates a sense of the safe comfort he'd experienced in the womb. And the quick "Shh, shh, shh …" of a mother's whisper sounds like the rhythmic beating of her heart.

In those early days, weeks, and months when my baby cried on and off, day and night, night and day, I would come to his aid. I lifted his agitated form up and out of the bassinet down the hall, wrapped him tightly, and held him securely in my arms. I bounced and swayed and shushed and sang until he relaxed into the safety net of my hold. His cheek pressed to my chest, lips slightly parted, pacifier barely holding on, I'd slowly move back to his bed and lay down my tiny inchworm again. Before leaving his room I'd adjust his pacifier and leave him in that swaddled embrace.

Today my oldest is thirteen years old, and his brothers are eleven and nine. Needless to say, I do not swaddle them, or rock them, or shush them to sleep anymore. And yet, there are plenty of times they still cry.

Plenty of times.

There are afternoons when one or all of them are stressed out emotionally, physically, or hormonally. And, if I'm being honest, it's quite inconvenient now. Their stressed out cries stress me out and make me want to cry. Throwing my hands in the air, I sigh. After all, we've been through this already. I taught them to "use your words" when they were toddlers. I consoled them and held them close when night terrors or growing pains attacked. I've done my job! Now here we are over a decade later and new tears threaten, sometimes on a daily basis.

Nearly all children cry, but some children cry a lot. They are sensitive hearts.

"He's riding my scooter and I told him not to!" Tears. "Homework isn't fair!" Tears. "Nobody played with me today. What's wrong with me?" Tears. "So-and-so said I'm fat." Tears. "But I don't want to go to music lessons tonight." Tears. "How come you get to use your phone but I can't have more video games?" Tears. "You said you were going to watch a movie with us tonight and now it's too late. YOU LIED!" More tears. "But we already had broccoli this week and I hate it. I hate it. I hate it ..." Tears. Tears. Tears. "Mom, I don't know what's wrong with me. I just feel sad." Tears.

Listen parents, our children will cry real, hot, salty tears in every single season of their growing up lives. Sometimes the reasons make sense to us—a broken arm or a broken heart—while other times the root of our child's emotional angst is as elusive as those first newborn cries. But, no matter the reason or the season, we want to be parents who care about our children's sorrows, just as our Father in heaven cares about ours.

> *"You keep track of all my sorrows. You have collected all my tears in your bottle. You have recorded each one in your book"* *(Psalm 56:8, NLT).*

We care, we do, but it's so easy to grow weary of the cries. "You've got to stop crying and get a handle on your emotions!" We blurt out with blame and shame when what they really need is to be swaddled up tight and whispered truth.

Whether the tears spring up from a deep reservoir of hurt or flood out of discontented hearts, our children cry out to us with real emotions, and it's our (on-going) job to walk them through every peak and valley and teach them how to calm themselves down as we sojourn by their sides.

When they are babies it's our job to soothe them, but as they grow up we must teach them to self-soothe.

When they are babies it's our job to soothe them, but as they grow up we must teach them to self-soothe.

So what should you say when these emotional meltdowns happen day-in and day-out? What's your script? How do you soothe an emotional child in a way that teaches him or her to self-soothe?

Teaching them to self-sooth doesn't mean we leave them by themselves to figure it all out. We teach our children mature life skills by sliding up close to them, almost like a swaddle, reminding them again of their mother's beating heart as we acknowledge their emotional pain. When we affirm their experiences and feelings, we are able to enter into their hurt and offer them the coping skills they will need for the rest of their lives.

PARENTING SCRIPT:

If you have a highly dramatic daughter, a sensitive son, or siblings who tirelessly hurt one another's feelings, I imagine you are tired of the emotional rollercoaster. This chapter's for you. Here are three steps I take when walking down the hall or across the playground to one of my children when he is crying … again. Each one of these steps includes some of my own script.

1. **Walk, don't run.**

    When you're emotionally wound-up child starts crying from their room or from the driveway, walk, don't run. Each calm, collected step communicates you care and are concerned, but you're confident that they will be alright. "I hear you … I'm coming," Is all you need to say. Perhaps there's a culprit, a child who hit or used unkind words. Don't address them right now. They can wait for you to parent them a little bit later. If however they are already screaming defensively, "It's not my fault," point them to their room and keep on walking ... slowly.

2. **Show empathy.**

"Sweetheart, are you okay?" Again, knowing that you care is key, before you offer them ways to soothe themselves. "That fall must have hurt..." "You must have been pretty upset with your friend ..." "You seem to be very stressed about the driving test / SAT / school dance..." Affirm their emotions. Let them know that you are on their team.

Move on.

When your children are very little, moving on might simply mean changing the subject, redirecting their play, or swaddling them in your arms then administering a tickle. But as they get older, "moving on" can include a bit of instruction. "Hey buddy, I can't understand you when you're crying. Can you tell me what's going on in a calm way? When you're calm you're always so good at coming up with a solution to your problem ..." "When your brother hurts your feelings, you are really good at forgiving him quickly ..." "When you calm down from being upset about having to do homework, you are always so quick and rarely get any math problems wrong ..." "When you have a problem with your friends and are able to take some time and think it through, you almost always come up with a really good way to talk it through with them. I'm always so proud of you and the way you deal with your hurts and fears once you calm down."

And finally, don't forget to swaddle them close. Even your great big man-child or your beautiful tween needs to remember the close, comforting sound of your heartbeat.

Sometimes our children's tears make us cry because we care so much, other times we're a weepy mess because we're so worn out by all the drama. Getting angry or simply shutting down and letting them "cry it out" is a common response on the other side of those baby years. After all, shouldn't they have learned to reign in their emotions by now?

No... their little brains are still so immature. They throw crying fits for goldfish at the grocery store and over one more storybook at bedtime because it all feels paramount in their little lives. Their minds are consumed, and the floodgates threaten to break. Likewise, your preteen's hormonal stress over first crushes and hurt feelings are equally difficult. **Empathy is key at every age and every stage.** Let's not grow weary of their cries. Stay calm, walk slowly, and gently swaddle them with care, concern, and kindness. And don't forget: when they cry for you, cry out to the Lord for help!

SCRIPT-URE:

"But in my distress I cried out to the LORD; yes, I prayed to my God for help. He heard me from his sanctuary; my cry to him reached his ears"

(Psalm 18:6, NLT)

PRAYER SCRIPT:

Dear Lord, we thank you for hearing our cries, and we trust You to comfort and minister to our children when they cry. Give us wisdom for how to respond in their emotional angst. And thank You for the way You gather our tears in a bottle, never growing weary with us in our weakness. We want to be more like You in this regard as well. Help us to love as You love. In Jesus' name, amen.

MAKE THE SCRIPT YOUR OWN:

Do you have a child who's prone to cry over every bump and bruise, or cry to be picked up and cuddled out of habit more than hurt? In the workbook pages, come up with a thoughtful and compassionate plan that honors their heart while helping them to mature into independent self-soothers.

Chapter 10 —
When Your Child
Disobeys

Amber

As a single woman, I loved holding babies. I even took great pride in getting the difficult ones to take naps, flopping list-lessly in my arms, little bow mouths gaping in contented restfulness. When my turn came along to cradle my own firstborn, he resisted naps like it was his job. I learned early on that our own kids aren't always going to cooperate. As he grew, it was an even bigger eye opener to see his perpetual tendency toward doing the exact opposite of what I asked him to do.

Disobedience, it seemed, came naturally. Psalm 58:3 says, "The wicked are estranged from the womb; they go astray from birth, speaking lies." I didn't need to teach my child to ignore my instructions or be deceitful. He instinctively knew how to sin. The terrible twos were especially cruel because they began at age one. Meanwhile, my friends who married and began families many years ahead of me were lamenting about the waywardness of their adolescents and teenag-ers. Sure, we loved our kids and experienced many happy moments of peace in our homes, but we needed a strategy to help them become obedient kids.

When our child stands before us, caught in disobedience, we often say nonsensical things like, "Why don't you listen to me?" and "When will you ever learn?" but these kinds of questions don't do any good, do they? They only serve to convey our frustration and disappointment. Or worse, belittle our children. If we resort to yelling at them, we sin ourselves and lose the opportunity to reach their hearts with our calm but thoughtful words. If only there were a magic wand that stops disobedient kids from continuing to do the wrong things over and over again. Instantaneous change is what we want, when really what we need to commit to is working with our kids toward obedience over the course of their childhood. We need to show them why it's in their best interest to do the right thing. The Bible makes these promises about obedience:

"My son, do not forget my teaching, but let your heart keep my commandments, for length of days and years of life and peace they will add to you" (Proverbs 3:1-2).

"A wise son heeds his father's instruction, but a mocker does not respond to rebukes" (Proverbs 13:1 NIV).

"Honor your father and mother" (this is the first commandment with a promise), *"that it may go well with you and that you may live long in the land" (Ephesians 6:2-3).*

If God emphasizes the benefits of obedience in His Word, then I better emphasize them in my parenting.

Four sons into my parenting journey, I've learned that shaping obedient kids has a lot to do with what I say to them and how I say it. There's one phrase in particular that almost always stops them in their tracks and causes them to make a right choice. But it goes a step beyond stopping unsavory behavior. I want the scripts I say to also help them grow, mature, and think about the effect of their actions. Christ needs to be mirrored in my attitude and words, even in the middle of a conflict. That's why I love this parenting script so much.

PARENTING SCRIPT:

Me: "What happens when you disobey?"

Child: "Things don't go well."

Sounds pretty simple, doesn't it? Though the script itself is only five words, the meaning behind it is loaded and profoundly truth-filled. This script takes some forethought and planning to implement. Before I began to use this script in such a way that my son could respond to me, I did some teaching and coaching. Allow me to explain with this example:

One day, my son chose to jump off a high wall in our yard. I warned him not to do so, but he disobeyed. Sure enough, he got mildly injured. The tears flowed while I held him close. Later on, in a time outside of conflict or emotional upheaval, we had a heartfelt talk about his decision to disobey me:

Me: "Son, the reason I told you not to jump from the high wall is because I knew it would not go well for you. I knew you would get hurt, and because I care for you so much I asked you to stop. You made a choice to disobey, and things didn't go very well, did they?"

Son: "No," he shook his head.

Me: "In the future, when I ask you the question, 'What happens when you disobey?' I want you to remember and respond that 'things don't go well.'"

Over the course of a few weeks, I gently but lovingly practiced this phrase with him, reminding him of Ephesians 6:2-3. Even after this line of conversation, sometimes he would willingly decide to make a move toward disobedience and as one last check I would gently say:

"So just to be clear, you are choosing to disobey right now? It's up to you, but I really hope you will choose to do what is going to go well for you, because I love you."

Nearly every time, that added question prompted him to think it through carefully and turn from the temptation after all. Whenever my boys make a right choice to resist temptation and do the right thing, I affirm them:

"I'm so glad to see you making a hard but good choice. Things will go well for you. You are honoring the Lord, Son. We are both pleased with you."

Parents need to be on the lookout for ways that their kids receive a blessing by obeying the Lord and quick to point out those benefits to them! On the flip side, when they shun our instructions, things certainly won't go well for them. If we have given clear expectations, our kids will know the fallout. Consequences should be loving, logical, and limited. If my sons value an object over their relationship with their sibling, and they fight and argue over it, they will most likely lose the privilege of playing with it. When they make a huge mess and ignore our instructions to help clean it up, they pay me from their allowance to do the job for them, and their wallets take a hit. If my teenager stays out beyond curfew, he understands that trust needs to be reestablished and a few more boundaries will be put into place, lessening his freedom.

Wouldn't it be amazing if our kids were so used to thinking about the impact of their actions that they turned into adults who instinctively evaluate their choices instead of being mastered by their desires or emotions? My prayer is that as my kids enter the various life stages from adolescence, to teenagers, to adults, that they will be skilled in thinking before they speak or act. This is the stuff of integrity—taking ownership for their choices and thinking carefully before heading down any wrong path. I also desire that they see the heart behind my desire for their good, and that God's love for them will compel them to do the right thing. Impulsivity must yield to maturity of mind, heart, and action. Our willingness to use parenting scripts gives them something to remember as much as it equips us to respond gently and biblically instead of in anger.

Parenting isn't just about raising great kids. It's always about the spiritual growth of mom and dad too. Every time I replay this script with my children, the added bonus is that I am reminded that in my own life, blessing will only follow my obedience. Each time I respond with gentleness, every moment I seek to draw the heart of my child with loving kindness, and each hour I choose to meditate on what is true and pure and lovely about being a mom, I am setting myself up for things to go well for me and to honor God.

It's been many years since those days of blissful ignorance of rocking someone else's baby to sleep and then heading home to the peace and quiet of my apartment. I wouldn't trade those carefree days for the entire world though. Our children are a gift and a treasure, but the sleeping giant of disobedience must be put to bed for good in order for them to experience the benefits of God's blessing in their lives, that it may go well with them, indeed.

SCRIPT-URE:

"My son, do not forget my teaching, but let your heart keep my commandments, for length of days and years of life and peace they will add to you"

(Proverbs 3:1-2)

PRAYER SCRIPT:

Father, thank You for giving us boundaries. I know You want Your children to obey so it will go well with us. I need this reminder as much as my children do. Please help me to be the kind of parent who is willing to take the time to teach and train my children with patience and understanding. Give my children obedient hearts that seek to do the right thing from a heart of love and a desire to honor me and You! Transform all of us, Father, that we may receive Your blessings and so it may go well with us. In Jesus' name, amen!

MAKE THE SCRIPT YOUR OWN:

In what situations do your kids tend to struggle with obedience the most? Where do you struggle with obeying God in your own life? What creative things can you do to teach, train, and coach your child toward obedience in a way that reaches their heart? In the workbook pages, write out your own script for disobedience that fits your own family dynamics.

Chapter 11 —
When They're
Melting Down Over
Homework / Homeschool

Wendy

I was a latchkey kid, collecting cute and colorful shoelaces to wear around my neck with a house key dangling at the end. On the days I forgot my necklace, I'd crawl through the window at the back of the house into my brother's bedroom. The lock on that window was perpetually broken.

As long back as I can remember, our house rules were simple: an hour of TV and then on to homework! So I'd hustle home to watch *Little House on the Prairie*, grab a snack, then do whatever schoolwork I had. Since I don't actually remember any consistent homework until Jr. High, I assume there wasn't much. I also don't have a single memory of my parents looking over my work or signing a contract about how many minutes a night I would read or practice my multiplication tables. School was different when we were kids, and parenting was different too.

Today there's a homework packet sent home with many kindergarteners each week, and parents are on top of every assignment! Grades are posted on websites for us to stay current on how many pages our student has read each quarter. We know everything that's happening in real time. There isn't one nag-free night assigned.

Now that my oldest is a teenager, I'm learning that my help doesn't always help him. Micromanaging our kids doesn't prepare them to manage their own lives. Our goal as parents is to work ourselves out of a job, and this is particularly true where study skills are concerned. It's more important that we help them to learn to learn than making sure they learned this week's particular spelling list. If they can take ownership and learn this week's lesson, then they can learn tomorrow's lessons too. However, most parents never pass the baton of responsibility to their kids.

This past year I noticed my oldest child never learned to study for a test. So instead of going through the specific material with him, I took the time to go over how to study. He learned to make index cards and study in preparation for finals. As we neared the end of the semester I asked him, "Do you know when your tests are, and do you have any study guides?"

He shrugged, shuffled, and sighed a phlegmatic, "I don't know."

I won't lie here in the pages of this book—my face turned hot and my temper flared. "What do you mean you don't know?" I began with more passion than compassion.

On the backside of that argument I realized two things: First, my child doesn't just need to learn to study, he needs to learn to care. And secondly, I shouldn't care so much! Don't get me wrong, we need to care for the sake of our children, but we don't need to care with such intense passion! This isn't our life, it's theirs. They need to learn for their own benefit, not ours. This isn't about us. **Parenting isn't about us.**

Our children aren't little miniatures of you and me, and God didn't intend for them to make us happy. He made them with their own passions and talents and learning styles, and even their own unique "good works" for them to discover and to walk in. (Ephesians 2:10.) Our job is to partner with the Lord to help guide them in the right direction on their quest to discover God's good plan.

PARENTING SCRIPT:

Because I'm prone to lecture and nag, my parenting scripts have to stay short and sweet. My children are familiar with this bite-sized admonishment: "This is your homework, your grade, your life. This is not my homework. You are welcome to ask me to help you with your homework, but do not wait for me to make you do it because it's not mine."

Though I don't have a college student yet, I know the time is coming. SATs will be upon us and college applications too. How will our children ever be ready to manage all of these wonderful responsibilities if we helicopter in and hold their hands through each assignment? "It's your homework, it's your grade, it's your life. You are welcome to ask me for help, but don't wait for me to make you do it because it's not mine."

Many parents look to Proverbs 22:6 when trying to prepare their children for a lifetime of faith, but I think it's full of application beyond their faith-life. "Train up a child in the way he should go; even when he is old he will not depart from it" (Proverbs 22:6). That phrase, "in the way he should go" is about their complete lives. Their lives. Not ours.

Since two of my children have some learning challenges, homeschooling was a great option for our family. It gave me the chance to consider their learning styles and even their bent, so to speak, and help aim them in the right direction. One of them has ADD and needs a quiet work environment. When his brain synapses aren't firing, I can encourage him to go outside and run a few laps or pick up his guitar and learn a new song. When he's feeling ready to learn, he sits down and tries again.

The other homeschooled kid tends to get stressed out over his school. I've learned that writing out his assignments on the same type of paper and in the same order each day helps him to feel calm and capable. While I personally love lots of fun extra assignments to bring a history lesson to life, complete with art assignments and poems and even fun recipes and movies, a more streamlined approach helps this particular child get through his work without meltdowns.

When we learn how they learn, we can teach them how to learn.

I've learned to learn my learners.

When we learn how they learn, we can teach them how to learn. Training them up in the way they should go is a lot easier when we understand their natural bent. The terminology used in this Scripture is often used in archery. Training them up in the way they are to go means knowing the unique curvature of each arrow so we can string it just right and shoot it just right so that it goes perfectly to the center of the bull's eye.

That's what we're after! Helping shoot them out of the nest and straight into God's good plan for their lives! The ultimate bull's eye of course is that they grow to be men and women who love Jesus with all their hearts... even if their study skills never do improve! Still, we are there to help them with both of these things.

Perhaps you agree with me, only your child throws a fit each and every time you call them to the table. I understand. My third kid, the one with afternoon homework, fights me like clockwork. Every day at 3:15 this child exclaims, "But I don't have any homework!" until he's blue in the face.

I used to chase him down with a handful of unfinished math pages fresh from his backpack. You see, his fit consistently caused me to throw a fit of my own! That is, until I wrote myself the parenting script I've already shared: "It's your homework, it's your grade, it's your life. You are welcome to ask me for help, but don't wait for me to make you do it because it's not mine."

Since this child is only nine, I found he needed a bit more help and firmer boundaries than his two older brothers, so I came up with an additional script, a sub-script, just for him:.

In the car on the way home from school (every school day) I say these same words: "Hey buddy, when we get home, before you play with your brothers, you're going to take your backpack into the house and bring your red homework folder to the kitchen table."

"But I don't have any homework!"

"Wonderful!" I reply with sincere joy, "that means you'll be able to play in no-time-flat! How awesome is that?"

I won't lie, Ladies, four times out of five that same kid makes it into the house and out through another door by the time I come to the kitchen table. His red folder and its contents strewn about the glass tabletop and onto the floor beneath.

While this used to make me upset and spout off at the mouth, now I remain calm and simply remember the second half of my new sub-script. Walking slowly to the back door (I don't even have to open it because the kid has left it wide open in his youthful exuberance to get to his afternoon fun), I walk out to where he is playing and call, "Asher, you need to come inside and show me the work you've brought home."

"But I don't have any homework!"

"That's fine," I say, remaining calm, "but you still have to take everything out of your folder, every day, and show it to me. Every day I will tell you the same thing, so you shouldn't be surprised. Every day you will do this same thing. And every day I will use a calm and kind voice, and you will respond respectfully."

One more trick I've learned when writing myself a better response: slipping scripts within the scripts helps me to remember who I am and how I speak to my children. If you look back through the dialogue with my son, you'll find these words, "... every day I will use my calm and kind voice, and you will respond respectfully." Just as I speak simple truth over my children, I need to speak truth over myself as well. Since I'm prone to react emotionally, I make sure I've penned plenty of calming mothering mantras to keep me from reacting in anger.

So let's choose our words carefully, moms and dads, the words we speak to them and the ones we say over our own hearts. Whether we're helping with homework or teaching our kids at home, it's a privilege to partner with the Lord and help send our kids off into the good works He has planned for them!

SCRIPT-URE:

"Train up a child in the way he should go; even when he is old he will not depart from it"

(Proverbs 22:6)

PRAYER SCRIPT:

Lord, would you please give me insight into how You made my children to learn? Grow in them a passion for learning that will last their whole lives! Give me the right words to speak over them, cheering them on, not shaming them to the table. I bless them and thank You for the good works you have planned for them. I want to partner with You, training them up in the way they are to go. In Jesus' name, amen.

MAKE THE SCRIPT YOUR OWN:

Is homework a struggle there in your home? Or perhaps you homeschool around your kitchen table. Either way it can be hard, because parenting is hard. But neither homework nor homeschool have to be our undoing. Consider what seems to be the same recurring problem day after day. In the workbook pages take some time to pen a better plan before the next school day rolls around with the same old struggles.

.

Chapter 12 —
When Your Child Needs to Show Brotherly (or Sisterly) Affection

Amber

Maya Angelou once said, "I don't believe an accident of birth makes people sisters or brothers. It makes them siblings, gives them mutuality of parentage. Sisterhood and brotherhood is a condition people have to work at." My family was divided before I was even born. My parents and older brother were raised in a strict separatist religious cult, and on one divinely appointed evening they were excommunicated, flung out into a world they considered evil. They were cast off like dust from a rug, discarded. Their grandparents, parents, siblings, cousins—left behind. It was into this tumultuous environment that I was born and that would forever shape my life.

Eventually, my family was invited to a sound Bible-teaching church. I was raised to memorize and recite weekly Scripture verses from toddlerhood until I went to college, and it was this intense abiding in the Word that would lead me to salvation at a young age and serve to guide me all the days of my life. In addition to a rich biblical knowledge at this church, my fractured family life found friendship that felt more like kinship. My aunties and uncles and grandmas and grandpas were never blood, but seemed just the same to me. Maya Angelou's words rang true for us. We had to work at sisterhood and brotherhood.

Now, as a mother myself of four wonderful boys, there are plenty of blood relatives to go around. Unfortunately, that doesn't necessarily make us family in the sense I dream of, because being born into a Christian home doesn't automatically make sibling relationships the stuff of dreams. I know I'm not the only mom who struggles to unite my children so they become the best of friends. My vision for family is the one I see laid out over the pages of God's Word. Every believer is compared to an integral part of a human body—the Body of Christ—each serving one another to fulfill a healthy body that functions to honor God. In Ephesians 4:16 Paul writes, "From whom the whole body, joined and held together by every joint with which it is equipped, when each part is working properly, makes the body grow so that it builds itself up in love."

Every Christ-follower is equipped with specific gifts and abilities that allow the Body to thrive—from teaching, to showing hospitality, to encouraging others to persevere. Furthermore, the family of Christ and our personal families would do well to follow the commands laid out in Colossians 3:14-16:

> *And above all these put on love, which binds everything together in perfect harmony. And let the peace of Christ rule in your hearts, to which indeed you were called in one body. And be thankful. Let the word of Christ dwell in you richly, teaching and admonishing one another in all wisdom, singing psalms and hymns and spiritual songs, with thankfulness in your hearts to God.*

PARENTING SCRIPTS:

That's all well and good to know, isn't it? But what in the world do we do when our children are fighting over who gets the first slice of cake or resorting to a fist fight when someone loses at a card game? What can we say that will cause them to have genuine affection for one another? The root of most sibling rivalry is pride. It requires an upheaval in the mind and the heart, away from self and toward loving sacrifice. Practically speaking, when my kids divide over positions or possessions, I ask them this simple question:

"What can you do to outdo?"

Romans 12:10 says, "Love one another with brotherly affection. Outdo one another in showing honor." As a family, we have examined this verse closely, breaking down what each quality means and how that might look among brothers and sisters in everyday moments. I want them to think less about what others can do for them and more about what they can do to outdo their brothers in honor and affection. **If we want adult children who love one another, they must become kids who practice it.**

If we want adult children who love one another, they must become kids who practice it.

It starts early at our house. The sun rises and the sons rise, and I hear their voices lilting down the hallway: "I was here first!" they argue as they jockey for the best position on the couch. There's no need to get exasperated and raise my voice. A simple, "What can you do to outdo, son?" and the argument dies down. One brother acquiesces his seat to another. In the afternoon, one brother complains that his brother got to go to the store with dad and he didn't. By evening, each of them wants to take their nightly bath first. Each time, not robotic, but with gentle sincerity, I ask them again, "What can you do to outdo?" I need the reminder too, as often as they do.

And then, over time, I observe them taking turns at the basketball hoop outside. I see smiling when they hear that one or the other gets to attend a birthday party and sharing what they appreciate about one another when the lights go out at bedtime. As the years go by, they are growing in inches and advancing in character.

One of Wendy's family mission statements says this, "We honor our parents, prefer our brothers, and encourage others." Preferring brothers (and sisters) is at the heart of brotherly kindness. It means wanting what's best for another before we take it for ourselves.

The beauty of this concept of outdoing one another in affection is that it's not meant for brothers and sisters by birth alone. Whether we have an only child or are parents of a dozen, we can use this approach to help our kids navigate friendships too. Imagine if we applied this idea to our marriages? To every relationship? It certainly does take work. Brotherhood and sisterhood aren't a given. Blood relationships don't become bonded relationships unless we put the effort into coaching our kids toward selflessness, placing the responsibility on them.

My past has left me with a strong desire to bind the hearts of my children to one another. I've known all too well the pain of splintered families. It's not God's plan for us in our homes or in the church to put ourselves and our desires before the needs of our brothers and sisters. *Outdoing one another cannot be outdone.* And in so doing, affection grows.

SCRIPT-URE:

"Love one another with brotherly affection. Outdo one another in showing honor"

(Romans 12:10)

PRAYER SCRIPT:

Lord, You designed families to be places where we learn what it means to love one another. Teach me how to be more intentional in coaching my family toward brotherly affection and honor. Soften the hearts of my children so they will be selfless with each other and grow up to be close friends who honor You by their relationship. Father, knit our hearts together by Your love. Heal the wounds that may hinder us from humility, and give us grace. In Jesus' name, amen.

MAKE THE SCRIPT YOUR OWN:

In what areas do you see a need for your kids to prefer one another? What's one thing they can do to outdo? What's one practical way you can coach them in this area? In the workbook pages, write out your own script for growing in brotherly affection and honor that fits your own family dynamics.

Chapter 13 —
During Bedtime Battles

Wendy

After a long day of pouring out love amidst constant correction and then finally tucking the children all tenderly into bed, you're done.

D. O. N. E. Done.

But then it starts. One or more of them crawls out of their warm covers and finds you folding the mountain of cold, wrinkled clothes on your bed. You'll never get to sleep at this rate, so you usher them quickly and quietly back to their room with a cool glass of water. That's when the whining begins in earnest. You never sang them the specific song they wanted or gave back tickles. You only cuddled and read a story and prayed a blessing over them. And they're afraid because you're all the way on the other side of the house in your room. "Can't you clean the kitchen with the light on, that way I know you're close?" The older sibling hears the commotion and comes out, "You're still up, mom? Good. Would you rub my legs? They're all cramped up and aching." And the baby starts to cry.

Are you stuck in a perpetual cycle of bedtime battles? Do you feel sick to your stomach just thinking about it?

I remember a long stretch when my husband was traveling for work, and the boys were all calling out or coming out of bed each night. One of those nights, when I was completely confident that they were all (finally) down, I walked myself down the hall to my bedroom, peeling off my dirty clothes en route. Turning on the shower I allowed the water to heat up first. I grabbed my toothbrush and squeezed a liberal dollop on the bristles then began to brush my teeth with eyes closed. The combination of steam from the shower and the minty-fresh toothpaste felt like victory at the end of another long day.

Then suddenly, I felt something brush against my hip (remember that I'm completely naked with my eyes closed), and I screamed. Throwing the toothbrush, I absolutely frightened the guts out of my middle boy who was now crying, traumatized. He whimpered, "I just needed to smell you one more time."

Oh my word!

I grabbed the towel, turned off the shower, and walked the child back to his bedroom—again. I'm pretty sure I fell asleep beside him after that, towel and all.

Needless to say, this is a script I desperately needed to write for myself. Without a plan, I was catching myself exploding harshly at my very young children, blaming and shaming them instead of teaching them to stay in their beds and go to sleep. Thinking of it now, this may have been the first time I actually wrote down a new response because what I was doing wasn't working. Depending on your children, whether they are mostly compliant but pushing boundaries, or strong-willed and pushing everything, I encourage you to find just the right response for your family. I tried a few until I found the one that worked (and continued to work) best for the boys and me. Here are a few to inspire you:

PARENTING SCRIPTS:

I have a child who is never satisfied with what he's given, from the number of cookies beside his glass of milk to the number of chapters I read to him at night. Always, he wants more or different. My tendency, over time, was to simply say no to him at the start of his nighttime routine. I was worn out before we even began because I knew that no matter how many yeses this child received from me, he would push until he got a tearful no!

Trouble was, I wanted to keep saying yes. I wanted my child to get cuddles and blessings and books and songs and cookies and back rubs ... he just couldn't have it all, all the time.

And so I started letting him choose.

"Hey buddy, good job being in bed with the lights off. Tell me two special things you'd like from me tonight. A back rub and a song? Or a chapter in your book and a little talk? Choose two things, and then I'll climb in beside you."

Another thing that worked with this kid, especially on days when he was discontent with what he already received, was to first ask him, "Can you tell me two amazing, wonderful things you already received from me today? Before I give you a tuck-in I want to hear what other things I did for you that made you feel loved." Sometimes he mentioned something special I cooked, like bacon. Other times it would be a trip to the park or a craft at the table. I found this simple question took the fight out of him. I'll share more about this tactic in a later chapter on discontentment, but I had to mention it here as well.

I've found that when having them list a couple of blessings they've already received, there's less of a fight for more and more once the lights are off. And if they do still want to fight, I remind them gently. "Hey buddy, you just told me two wonderful things we enjoyed today. And then you got the sweet tuck-in that you chose. Your little heart should be soooooo full, you don't need one more thing. Let me hear you say 'I don't need one more thing ...'"

"I don't need one more thing."

After a while he knew our routine and was prepared to share his two blessings from the day and request his two bedtime blessings.

Another child had bedtime anxiety and needed Scripture songs and a spray of lavender on his pillow in order to calm down (and stay down.) He also needed to have his light left on until he fell asleep. Which, for some reason, bothered me no end. For years I fought him over this silly little thing. If I could go back and do things differently, I would never have made this a battle.

Sometimes bedtime battles are battles because we let them be.

My favorite parenting analogy is a game of tug-of-war. Remember, in that battle, if you drop your end of the rope, there's no one for your little opponent to fight. Is there anything (like a request to leave a light on) that you could say yes to? Drop your side of the rope. Go on and give it a try.

This last piece of advice is my favorite of all, and, again, I wish I had started it earlier on myself. And the best part is that it first came out of my husband's mouth and ended up being exactly what we all needed to help catapult us all out of the miserable cycle we'd gotten ourselves into. He simply said, "Boys, you're taking advantage of your mom each night. She's loved you well all day long, and now she's said goodnight. It's done now. If you come out or call out one more time, I will not let her tuck you into bed tomorrow. You may come to her for a hug, but she will not come into your room to say goodnight. Do you understand?"

Moms and dads, if you follow through with this consistently, they will learn.

SCRIPT-URE:

"Therefore, as God's chosen people, holy and dearly loved, clothe yourselves with compassion, kindness, humility, gentleness and patience. Bear with each other and forgive one another if any of you has a grievance against someone. Forgive as the Lord forgave you. And over all these virtues put on love, which binds them all together in perfect unity"

(Colossians 3:12-14, NIV)

PRAYER SCRIPT:

Lord, thank You for the gentle way You deal with me, in my ongoing willfulness. You never grow weary in extending grace toward me, and I want to be more like You at bedtime. Help me to understand how to communicate with my children as the sun goes down. What natural consequences will help them to learn to obey me at bedtime, and how can I keep saying yes to love, rather than no in anger? You are my best example of what a loving parent looks like, Lord. Thank You.

MAKE THE SCRIPT YOUR OWN:

Do you have kids who keep getting out of bed each night? This is one of those struggles that moms and dads need to work out together if there are two parents in the same house.

Find a moment together when there is not conflict, and consider anew what their bedtime routine might look like if you tried something different. Then write it down, in the workbook pages.

Chapter 14 —
When Your Child
Hurts Your Feelings

Amber

She was your average teenage girl, doing her best to be covert about the note she was writing to a friend instead of listening to my lecture on William Golding's *Lord of the Flies*. Little did she know that I saw her scribbling away, pretending to write down the themes of the novel, when in reality she was offering up some juicy bits of dirt to her tenth grade class-mate. I couldn't help but inwardly cringe at the irony. The animalistic behavior of the little boys on a deserted island was Golding's way of revealing that the heart of man is not as innocent as we would like to believe. In truth, we can turn savage in a moment, tearing others down for our own gain. Within the confines of civilization, the heart of man bleeds just as darkly in the form of high school gossip.

The bell rang and as my student packed her bags I calmly asked her to place the note on my desk before she went to lunch. She set some random schoolwork from another class in front of me, trying to pass it off.

"Oh no, Laura. Not these. The note you were writing to Krista. The one with the flowers doodled on the right side," I said calmly.

Her face went pale as she realized I had called her bluff. She tried to protest but changed her mind when I calmly explained to her that if she didn't comply, I would simply walk with her to pay a visit to the dean. After she reluctantly handed the note over and went on her way, I unfolded the crumpled letter and discovered why she was so averse to giving me the note. The main subject was me. She guffawed over my outfit, said a few unsavory words about her homework assignment, and ended the note with one final zinger aimed at making herself look cool by making an obscene observation about me. I was pretty surprised. While this student wasn't the warm and fuzzy type, I had no idea the layers of ugliness that festered in her heart. It was discouraging for sure, but I took it all in stride. As a veteran teacher working with high schoolers, I realized that Laura's note had very little to do with me and much more about her own feelings of self-consciousness and teenage need to feel accepted by others. I didn't spend too much time lamenting that I wasn't her favorite adult. In fact, I went out of my way to show her kindness in the days that followed, though her shame spoke for her as she often avoided me.

But then there came a day when teaching was long behind me, and I became a mother to four little boys. I endured years of painful pregnancies and infections from breastfeeding, sacrificed my own desires to care for their every need, and lavished more love than I knew a body could pour out on another human being. Of all the titles I have ever worn, the one I felt I earned the most, by sheer outpouring of myself, was mom. As invested as I was as a teacher, those days paled in comparison to the commitment I made to loving and raising my children to one day become godly adults.

Once the smiling and cooing stages of babyhood morphed into toddlerdom and beyond, I imagined that my children would always speak respectfully to me and appreciate all I did for them as their parent. After all, they are my people! But then it happened. My own kids dared to say awful things to me in moments of deep frustration and immature meltdowns. "I don't love you anymore!" they would wail. "You are so mean!" and "I don't want you to be my mom!" they would pout. I even heard an "I hate you!" a time or two.

How could this be? I wondered, wounded. *Don't they realize all I do for them?* Their words pelted the surface of my heart like splinters. I know teenagers can be mouthy, but what in the world did my five-year-old have so much to be upset about that he would say such a thing? And then I remembered. I remembered my own searing words toward my mom and dad when I was that age. All those untamed feelings that I didn't know how to handle, poured out of my young mouth. I remember feeling immediately sorry I had said them, because in truth, I didn't mean them. If only my mom had enfolded me in her arms and said this:

PARENTING SCRIPT:

"I don't think you mean that."

If my child says something that threatens to hurt me to the core, I have learned to say this one healing phrase. When I tell my children I don't believe them, they may very well retort that they do mean what they said, but that's just another opportunity for me to reassure them that I simply don't accept it. In fact, I know that they love me and they are just frustrated. I go on to say, "Besides, nothing you do or say could ever change my love for you. I love you right now, even in this moment." When I challenge his angry words, and reassure him of my unconditional love, I can literally see my little guy's body relax under the relief that he hasn't hurt me after all. He's safe again to let the walls of resentment come down so we can move toward a loving reproof. I see the chink in his armor give way when I remove that unsavory piece of the conflict—that question about his feelings for me. Then, and only then, am I in a place to get to the root of the issue at hand. Perhaps he needs some teaching and training in contentment or obedience, but at least we don't have to add an emotional tug-of-war of heightened feelings because of his careless words and my own sensitivity.

The truth is, when our kids say hurtful things to us, they regret it, just like we do. Ecclesiastes 7:21-22 says, "Do not take to heart all the things that people say, lest you hear your servant cursing you. Your heart knows that many times you yourself have cursed others." Gulp. Haven't you said things you didn't mean? Even recently, perhaps? Sure. We all do this at times—at least most of us do. We have an out-of-body experience, if you will, as we hear ourselves saying the things we never imagined we might say. The shame washes over us before we have even closed our lips. But oh, to get caught! That would be awful. And yet, if I did get caught—like my student was caught, like my children have been caught—what a balm it would be to have someone not take me at my word when my untamed tongue let loose. What grace we experience when someone looks beyond the moment and believes the best about us in spite of ourselves. That's what I want us to do for our children.

Godly parenting is countercultural. The world would have us believe that we are always justified to take revenge, to pay people back for any harm they do toward us. We use our car horns to let drivers know what we think about their lack of road skills, and we scratch someone's back only when we can be sure they will at some point satisfy our own itch. If our children talk to us with disrespect, then we have every right to dish it right back and become defensive and hurt, putting them in their place. Or do we?

"I therefore, a prisoner for the Lord, urge you to walk in a manner worthy of the calling to which you have been called, with all humility and gentleness, with patience, bearing with one another in love, eager to maintain the unity of the Spirit in the bond of peace" (Ephesians 4:1-3).

If Jesus died to rescue our kids from hell, we shouldn't give them hell to pay on earth. God wouldn't charge us to "bear with one another in love" if there was not cause. When I refuse to take my child's unkind words personally, reminding him that I know that he really does love and care for me, I'm maintaining "the unity of the Spirit in the bond of peace" and showing him he doesn't need to resort to such unkind words. They won't work on my anyway.

If Jesus died to rescue our kids from hell, we shouldn't give them hell to pay on earth.

"I don't think you mean that," I gently but confidently say. No need to fall apart in a heap of martyrdom and self-pity. Moments like these allow me to show my child the kind of lavish grace—that undeserved merit—that Jesus so often bestows on me. It gives me a chance to remind him of who he really is, a child who is filled with strong emotions, who makes mistakes, but who is unconditionally loved. And I remind myself who I am, an adult whose role is to help my children navigate their grievances, bearing with them in their immaturity, whether they are three years old or fifteen.

Brush off those hasty words, parents. Don't allow them to penetrate your heart. Go a step further to right the wrong of your child by blessing them instead of cursing them (Luke 6:27-28). "I don't think you mean that," we say. And the meaningfulness of the moment builds a bridge from their hearts to ours, a godly picture of what Christ's love has done for us.

SCRIPT-URE:

"I therefore, a prisoner for the Lord, urge you to walk in a manner worthy of the calling to which you have been called, with all humility and gentleness, with patience, bearing with one another in love, eager to maintain the unity of the Spirit in the bond of peace"

(Ephesians 4:1-3)

PRAYER SCRIPT:

Lord, I confess that I often say things I regret. Help me to keep a guard over my own mouth so I only say what gives life to others and encourages them. Make this especially true when I speak to my child. Give me a heart that is not overly sensitive; rather give me a heart that is full of mercy and grace. Help me not to take my children's words personally, but to always bless them instead of curse them. Guide me as I teach them to use kind words and to manage their emotions in appropriate ways! Thank You, Lord, for being with me so I'm not trying to parent in my own strength. I will trust You for healing and guidance in my relationships in my home. In Jesus' name, amen!

MAKE THE SCRIPT YOUR OWN:

When does your child resort to hurtful words? What is it about this situation that sets them off, and how can you be proactive to help them handle their emotions? What do you need to remember when you are tempted to take their unkind words too seriously? In the workbook pages, write out your own script for when your child hurts your feelings that fits your own family dynamics.

Chapter 15 —
When Your Children Sin

Wendy

I tucked the youngest into bed. At eight years old, he's often exhausted before his older brothers and falls easily to sleep. Trusting he wouldn't need me again, I left the older two with their books and took myself to the bathroom down the hall to finally get a quiet shower before another day slipped by.

Unfortunately, when I opened the door and the steam lifted, I found my older two children in tears with the youngest strutting around the house like a bully on a playground. He had come out and said the most horrific things I'd ever heard one child say to another! I was heartbroken, alongside the brothers. However, I did not respond by bullying the bully. **Bullying a bully never changes them. Only love.**

Does that resonate with you? So often we jump into the fray with our kids and cry at their crying, holler at their hollers—trying to overcome their evil with our bigger and uglier evil rather than with good. I didn't do that this time because I had made a better plan to not respond aggressively when they've used aggressive words.

Bullying a bully never changes them. Only love.

Quickly and quietly I took him by the hand and led him back to his room.

With the sound of his older brothers crying in the distance, half muffled beyond this youngest child's bedroom door, I sat with him on his bed and allowed the silence to do a work in his heart. I remembered my commitment not to say anything immediately after a huge offense, and gave the Holy Spirit ample room to convict.

In the silence on his bed, I thought of the personal emails I get from moms and dads asking for words to speak when their children curse and cuss and are unkind to one another. Ugly words and awful tones plague many homes today, but up until that night, we had never had a child speak that way. Needless to say, I didn't have a good response in my arsenal of Parenting Scripts. I wasn't prepared. So instead of improvising, I sat and thought.

When my boy finally turned his huge eyes on me, I didn't see repentance or remorse reflected back. In calm and calculated tones I finally spoke, "I would never let anyone speak that way to you, and I will not let you speak that way to my other children. Your dad and I will be talking this through together, and there will be a very significant discipline for you, but I don't know what it is tonight."

"Will I get to go to my Christmas concert tomorrow night?" He asked with a tear (his first tear of the night, I might add.)

He has been working for months on his Christmas songs with the elementary school choir and was looking forward to the next day's big celebration. He was over the moon excited about this Christmas concert!

I shrugged with a sigh and said with a soft voice, "I don't know. It simply doesn't make sense that you would stand in front of

CHAPTER 15

the whole school singing praises to God only to come home and curse your brothers with the same mouth." That was when his tears finally let loose, and I held him as he cried.

After the children were finally asleep I thought of the verse that had echoed in my own words: "From the same mouth come blessing and cursing. My brothers, these things ought not to be so" (James 3:10).

Late into the night I pondered those words with my husband. Together we made a plan of what to say and how to discipline our youngest child. In the morning, with plan in place, I was up and dressed before our little antagonist awoke. Purpose-fully, I entered my child's room with good news to share. Actually, it was more than simply good news, it was the Good News.

I roused him from his slumber with a gentle back rub and opened up James 3:10, "From the same mouth come blessing and cursing. My brothers, these things ought not to be so."

I closed the good book and applied the good news this way:

PARENTING SCRIPT:

"Do you remember last night when I told you it doesn't make any sense for you to go sing praises to God at school and then walk around cursing your brothers at home?"

He nodded his head.

"Well, I was wrong. You can do that—and all of us do. This is why we all need a Savior. Sweet boy, you sinned big-time last night, and the way I see it, there's no better time to celebrate our need for a Savior than at Christmas."

Again the nodding head and expressive eyes.

"Speaking of your sin, when you were younger you asked Jesus to forgive all your sins and come live inside your heart. Do you remember that?"

"Yes."

"Well, since you were only five at the time, you didn't have a lot of sin in your life that you could see. The Bible tells us that above all else our hearts are sinful, and out of our hearts come sinful words and actions. So now that you're older, you see that you really do need His forgiveness. Son, this is the good news. Jesus was born and lived a perfect life, without sin. When He died on the cross, He didn't die for His own sin, He didn't have any. He did it for you, for your hurtful words last night. He took all the punishment that you deserve, and let it fall entirely upon Himself, so you could be forgiven. Forever, completely forgiven. That's the good news, son."

"Does that mean I won't be punished?" He asked, eyes even wider than before.

I couldn't help but laugh. "The punishment that God was talking about was hell—a forever separation from God. If you believe Jesus took your punishment for you, you won't have to be separated from God forever. However, I think you still need to be separated from your brothers for a while this morning. I'll call you when it's breakfast time. Spend some time thinking about what you need to say to them. Plan your words, just like I planned what I wanted to say to you. Be sure to ask for their forgiveness, because while God has forgiven you, your brothers still need to."

"And tonight I can go to the concert?"

"Yes, tonight you may go sing praises to the Lord at the Christmas concert! And, perhaps, you will praise Him more than ever, because last night you sinned and this morning you understood the good news—why Jesus, the Son of God, had to be born for your sake and mine."

Moms and dads, this Parenting Script isn't just for cussing and cursing, but for all ugly sins your children commit in their hearts and in your home. **The goal is the gospel, always. Every sin needs a Savior, and every child needs a parent to point them to Him.** The key is pulling back to plan the right response.

So often when we slow down, the Holy Spirit stirs up in us just the right words. Here are some of His Words, that you may want to hide in your heart for just the right time, when they need the gospel most of all.

> *"All have sinned and fall short of the glory of God" (Romans 3:23).*
>
> *"For the wages of sin is death, but the gift of God is eternal life in Christ Jesus our Lord" (Romans 6:23).*
>
> *"But God demonstrates His own love for us in this: while we were still sinners Christ died for us" (Romans 5:8, NIV).*
>
> *"For by grace you have been saved through faith. And this is not your own doing; it is the gift of God" (Ephesians 2:8).*
>
> *"Believe in the Lord Jesus, and you will be saved" (Acts 16:31).*

SCRIPT-URE:

"But God demonstrates His own love for us in this: while we were still sinners Christ died for us"

(Romans 5:8, NIV)

PRAYER SCRIPT:

Lord, we want to care more about our children's eternal salvation than we do their present sin struggles. Give us the eyes to see their sin as an opportunity to share Your gospel of salvation with them, gently, graciously. Thank you for taking our sin upon that cross too, Lord. Help us to respond to our children with compassion when they sin, knowing that we ourselves are simply sinners saved by Your grace. In Jesus' name, amen.

WRITE YOURSELF A SCRIPT:

Is there some sin in your child's life that needs correcting right now? **Ask God to inspire you how to use that specific sin-struggle as a doorway through which to walk your children to salvation and from there to transformation.** We want to be ready in season and out of season to share the good news with our kids. Look up the verses I've included, commit them to memory, and ask the Lord for opportunities to lead your children to Him. In the workbook pages, I encourage you to write yourself a gospel script.

Chapter 16 —
When Your Child
Is Lazy

Amber

For many months now, I have been implementing a new cleanup routine with my sons. Some of them are more willing to jump in to help than others, but one particular son would rather have his teeth drilled than pick up dirty cups and straighten his bedroom. All the tricks I used to make it fun, like mimicking a disco routine while we shimmy from room to room, picking up toys as we go, or timing them for a speedy sock pairing contest, weren't cutting it as far as he was concerned. The mirrored ball had lost its luster, and he wasn't buying into my lighthearted attempts to make work fun. He complained every time. Not just the mumble grumble type. More like the wailing-and-contorting-of-body-in-protest type.

In preparation of asking him to help around the house, I had to take deep breaths, bracing myself for the resistance. It was irritating, I'll be honest, but instead of punishing him or lecturing him about his complaining ways, which wasn't reaching his heart, I decided to allow him to whine his way through obeying me. His heart wasn't happy, but he was getting the job done. God often requires hard obedience from me. It's not always a happy thing to obey, but God wants us to do the right thing anyway. Bearing our cross is often an agonizing experience. If we can teach our kids to obey, even when they don't feel happy about it, we are instilling in them a seed of character that is deeply valuable and deeply Christlike. Meanwhile, as opportunities presented themselves in natural settings, I gently began teaching him about contentment and serving others. The issue at hand wasn't the misery he spewed over cleanup time, it was the gnarly root of discontentment and laziness that needed to be pruned. My script became my gardening sheers. Sometimes it sounded like this:

PARENTING SCRIPT TO FOSTER CONTENTMENT AND A STRONG WORK ETHIC:

"You know, son, as I stand here husking corn, I don't really enjoy it. It hurts my hand a bit, and it's a lot of mess to clean up. But I know how much your brother loves this corn, so it makes me happy to do it for him. It's a way I can serve him lovingly."

"Son, I know that not being chosen for that job in your classroom is a disappointment, but I like how you are doing the job you were assigned anyway."

"Hey, did you see how that main character in the show you were just watching handled that situation with his sister? She got the part in the play she wanted, but he didn't. He could have lashed out and complained, but instead, he was kind and gracious. I like that, and I think God does too. In fact, that character reminds me a lot of you. I'm proud of you when you are content and willing to help others, but I love you no matter what."

"Hey boys, come over here and look out the window. See your dad? Look how he's scooping up the dog mess in the backyard.

That's your job, but he's out there doing it for you just because he loves you. I bet you'll grow up to work sacrificially, just like your daddy does."

In Philippians 2:14 we see God desires us to "Do everything without grumbling or arguing" (NIV). The ultimate goal is to become blameless and pure hearted Christ-followers. I often have to examine my own motives here. I want my child to stop complaining because it's annoying to me, not because I want him to become more like Jesus. But when I shift my focus to what is best for my son—becoming godlier in character—my responses to his sinfulness are far more empathetic. I become more willing to recognize that his growth takes time. His sin is just that—his sin. I don't have to take it personally.

In our book, *Triggers: Exchanging Parents' Angry Reactions for Gentle Biblical Responses*, I remind parents that it takes a childhood to raise a child. Some issues my kids will face may take a very long time to improve. If I choose to be long-suffering with them, I'm going to have to be patient with the process of allowing the Holy Spirit to shape their hearts. I can wait it out, allowing the Holy Spirit to influence my child's thought life in His perfect timing. That's far more meaningful than forcing him to appear happy about tasks so I feel better.

After several months of speaking this script about laziness and contentment into my son's life, I noticed a significant change. As we went around the house, depositing trash in the bin, folding clothes and putting them into drawers, and sweeping up the incessant dog hair, my son who has been not so helpful as of late, quietly and efficiently went about the business of pitching in without one frown or grimace. About half way through our fifteen minutes of power cleaning I stopped and touched his arm to say, "Son, I see you working hard and doing it with a good attitude. I notice. Thank you for being so helpful." He nodded his head with a smile and carried on with the task at hand.

Painting a positive picture of who our kids can become motivates them in ways our disappointment never can. I fostered the maturing process, as messy as it often was, without damaging our relationship because of angry yelling or words spoken in frustration. Kids need our consistency, our prayers, and our willingness to teach them outside of conflict, allowing them to make choices for themselves. I could have punished him into plastering a smile on his face while he wiped down the bathroom counters, but it would have been an empty and meaningless coercion. The genuine smile and willingness to help me out of his own transformed heart is the kind of long-term change I want to develop in my kids. It was well worth the wait.

Painting a positive picture of who our kids can become motivates them in ways our disappointment never can.

Jesus is our perfect example of a servant: "For even the Son of Man came not to be served but to serve, and to give his life as a ransom for many" (Mark 10:45). My own ability to excise the laziness from my child's heart will be short lived if I'm not submitting the parenting process to the Lord in prayer. Who better to aide us in our desire to shape helpful kids than the ultimate Helper? If Jesus was willing to give His very life for us, surely He is also standing by, ready to guide us as we parent our kids.

If there is an issue your child is battling, like talking back, being lazy, or complaining, commit to praying about the best way to lovingly correct him or her and take opportunities to be an encouragement in this struggle. Approaching correction with empathy and understanding is far more effective than grim punishments or just ignoring the behavior and hoping it will get better someday.

The scripts we prepare for our kids don't always have to be spoken as a correction. Sometimes, our scripts are best implemented as positive lessons in everyday, organic moments when we can bless our children by our words.

My son's struggle to grow in contentment and to serve his family with gladness was about as messy as his room, but we are on our way to lasting change that is all the more wonderful because it stems from a willing heart.

SCRIPT-URE:

"Do everything without grumbling or arguing"
(Philippians 2:14, NIV)

PRAYER SCRIPT:

Heavenly Father, I confess that I often have a discontented spirit and that I don't always choose to serve others from a pure heart. Forgive me and change me. Allow my own growth toward contentment and joy to be a powerful example to my child. Thank You, Lord, for being the perfect example of humility, choosing to leave the kingdom of heaven to enter this world as a frail human being because You love me. May my child grow up to be like You—willing to lay down his/her life for others, and use me to show them the way. In Jesus' name, amen!

MAKE THE SCRIPT YOUR OWN:

Take a few minutes and reflect on your attitude as a parent. Do you want your kids to work hard and with a happy spirit because it's easier for you, or because you want them to become godly kids? Is there a little bit of both mingling in your heart? What approach can you take that would show a sense of compassion and intentionality as you help them grow in the area of service to others? In the workbook pages, write out your own script for lazy kids that fits your own family dynamics.

Chapter 17 —
On Your Worst Day

Wendy

It was 6:00 pm and the temperature outside was sweltering, hanging like a heat lamp somewhere between 107-109 degrees. The woman sitting on the park bench on my right was drinking what remained of her child's melted slurpee. When we made eye contact she moaned, "My kids have been out of control today. Absolutely wild. Bouncing from room to room. And they wanted to eat all day too. If I spent one moment cleaning something up, they were making an even bigger mess somewhere else in the house. It was chaos." A few other parents grunted in agreement.

We weren't "friends," just a ragtag group of parents, but we were comrades in the trenches at the end of a long day, in the middle of a long week, at the end of a hot summer.

In Southern California from mid-August through September we often get something called "The Santa Ana Winds" that blow like a furnace off the desert and toward the ocean. The Santa Anas were blowing that day. Once the sun was low enough in the sky, moms and dads and kids made their way to the park after a day pent up inside.

It was then that a dad walked up and sat down next to us, and we groaned again. Perhaps he'd brought some of the heat off of the parking lot asphalt, and we felt it collectively. A brother and a sister ran up to him and dropped their water bottles and scooters at his feet. They were squealing together and the sound made me squint. Their dad looked like he was on the verge of heatstroke as he took a long swig from a pink water bottle. "They've been making that noise all day," he sighed his apology.

"Blame it on the heat" the mom said between slurps.

With the dad on my left and the slurpee mom on my right, I felt like a grilled cheese sandwich, melted by the heat radiating off of them both. As I sat sandwiched between the two, I thought of Proverbs 17:22, "A joyful heart is good medicine, but a broken spirit dries up the bones" (NASB). There was more to these weary parents than heat exhaustion. I knew it from experience. I was surrounded by dry bones. I didn't feel critical of their complaints; I understood. My own kids' hyperactivity that morning and all of my attempts to redirect them to happy contented play had worn me out as well.

I should have planned a playdate. I should have planned a trip to Grandma's. I should have planned a trip to the beach. I should have planned.

I'd tried crafts and books and ran the sprinklers in an attempt to run the wiggles right out of them, but nothing worked. Unfortunately, I was worn from redirecting their rowdy by the time they started throwing all of the stuffed animals and dress-up clothes out of the closet I'd just organized. **I had been so calm and kind all day, until I wasn't.**

I had been so calm and kind all day, until I wasn't.

Suddenly, their roughhousing got under my skin and rattled my nerves. Before I knew it, I got rough right back at them.

"There was a lot of yelling in our house today," I confessed to the group of strangers.

"You just heard my kids yelling," said the dad.

"I was talking about myself," I said. And they laughed. Only it wasn't funny. It's never funny when we lose our cool ... even when it's hot. But we laughed because it's common, and what else could we do? Except, maybe, make the choice to not do it.

"My kids were out of control today too, don't get me wrong, but I'm the adult." I was preaching to myself, but the other parents were in earshot. "I hollered at them and complained, and then I complained and hollered some more."

A grandma at the bench next to ours lowered her phone and looked my way. "Tomorrow's supposed to be another scorcher," she warned me with a gentle voice.

"Which means I have about twelve hours to figure out what I'm going to do differently."

This story took place about five years ago, when the kids were four, six, and eight, and I was still suffering from a sad and complicated case of prolonged postpartum depression and hormonal imbalance mixed with adrenal fatigue. My nerves were shot, and I wasn't coping well.

Oftentimes I'd go to bed exhausted, feeling like a failure as I looked back over my day. "I should have ... I could have ... why didn't I?" My husband would reach over and gently stroke my hair out of my wet face, "Honey, go to sleep, God's new mercies will be waiting for you in the morning." He was referring to this sweet verse:

"The steadfast love of the Lord never ceases;
his mercies never come to an end;
they are new every morning;
great is your faithfulness"

(Lamentations 3:22-23)

The trouble was, I'd often gather up those blessed new mercies and do the same wrong things all over again. That is, until I learned to make a better plan. Parents, the goal here isn't perfection, Jesus is the only perfect One. But with His help we can make progress, and progress often starts with a plan.

There on the bench that day I didn't yet know what I was doing, but I knew I had to do something different. I knew I needed to use the Lord's allotted new mercies each day and spend them better than I had the day before. So I picked up my phone and sent a group text to some friends: "Who wants to meet up at the beach tomorrow? I have a case of water bottles and a ton of grapes I can freeze and put in the cooler"

Almost immediately my phone signaled a message: "I've got two boxes of Capri Sun, a bag of pretzels, and some Sunchips. How about Moonlight Beach at 10:00 am?"

Then another notification: "Halleluiah. We're in. Hard day. You're the best. I'm melting … and my kids have lost their minds! Also, I don't have anything to share but my brilliant personality. I'd make cookies, but then I'd have to turn the oven on."

As my children played on the swings and the slide (both which burned their bottoms), I made a practical plan for the next day, but I also had the brilliant idea to make a plan about how I was going to get them back into the car at the end of our beach day tomorrow. The last couple of times we'd gone anywhere, getting them back into the car was a nightmare!

I had friends who would bribe their children with lollipops once buckled in, and others who would carry multiple kids at once. Neither of these worked for me. So after I'd made a plan for our day at the beach, I started considering how I'd get us all into the car with positive words and happy hearts. Here's what I came up with (five years ago) that we still use today.

PARENTING SCRIPTS:

When it was time to leave the park, I was so excited about my plan, I decided to try it out on my kids right away. I called them over and they came with sweaty red faces. After dousing them with water from my bottle, I passed out their own then said, "I have an idea you guys! I have an idea that only the best mom in the entire world could come up with!" They laughed and begged to know what it was. "We're going to practice it tonight, and if we love it, we'll try it again tomorrow … on our way home from the beach!"

"We're going to the beach? Tomorrow? Seriously? Are Miles and Everett coming? Are Jake and Kate coming? You *are* the best mom!"

"Yes, but that's not the fun part! The fun part is how we're going to get in the car and go home now, and how we're going to get in the car after the beach tomorrow."

"How?" They asked.

"I'm so glad you asked. We're going to play DJ dance party."

"Huh?"

"From now on, whenever we need to get into the car, everybody who grabs their things and gets into the car with a happy heart, gets to choose the music on the way home. If you all make it into the car without a fit, you get to pass my phone around taking turns and playing DJ!"

In an instant, all three of them had grabbed their water bottles and were running for the car. The littlest one was in the lead shouting, "Jesus Freak, Jesus Freak! I'm going to choose Jesus Freak!"

Dear moms and dads, I love this story because I was up to my sad little adrenal glands in exhaustion that day, making the same old mistakes I'd probably made the day before. But it ended with this fun stroke of inspiration because I took the time and made a better plan.

These were some of my worst days as a parent. I often had a broken spirit and my bones felt mighty dry. Spiritually speaking, the Santa Anas had nearly blown me over. Still, I was able to make a fun plan to get us out of the house and into some play the next day. And then I made a plan to try a different way to get three gnarly little darlings into the car at the end of the fun as well. If I could do it on one of my worst days, I know you can do it too.

Perhaps you're stuck in a rut, living through some of your worst parenting days right now. Let me encourage you, God's mercies are waiting for you tomorrow, but it's up to you what you're going to do with them. Will you pick them up and misappropriate them all over again, or make a plan to enjoy them with your children?

SCRIPT-URE:

"The steadfast love of the Lord never ceases;
his mercies never come to an end;
they are new every morning;
great is your faithfulness"

(Lamentations 3:22-23)

PRAYER SCRIPT:

Dear Lord, You are so faithful to meet me in my mess and clean me up and put me to bed each night. What grace! Then You wake me up to the sun shining and the birds singing with rest in my heart. What mercy! Day after day, You are faithful, even when I'm faithless. It's simply too wonderful. And so I'm asking You today, help me to take Your grace and Your mercy and live them out with my kids. I don't want to sin against them again and again, though Your grace never runs out. Holy Spirit, won't you help me? I want Your grace to transform me and Your new mercies to inspire me as I make a plan for tomorrow.

MAKE THE SCRIPT YOUR OWN:

Imagine your worst day. What's the recurring theme there in your home? Come up with a plan to spend the Lord's new mercies better. Or, perhaps, you'd like to use the workbook pages to plan out how you want to try to get your kids into the car at the end of playdates or in the morning when it's time to head to school. Talk it through with the other parent in your home if you have one, and make a plan.

Chapter 18 —
When It's the Weekend

Amber

We had been up for an hour and a half but it didn't take long before two brothers were fighting over a game they were playing. "Moooommm, so and so did this or that!" they wailed. "You are such a jerk!" one screeched. And then there was the meltdown over scrambled eggs. Because we put bacon in them. *Heaven forbid*. Aren't Saturday mornings supposed to be lazy, refreshing, and fun? Instead, the lack of routine, the anticipation of a day all to ourselves, and the close proximity of siblings had everyone on edge. These weekend moments are *triggers*.

This particular morning came on the heels of an overly busy and stressful week. I was battling a little sadness about a relationship with a friend. I just wanted a peaceful morning at home where we could all enjoy one another and take a break from the demands of the week. The kids' squabbles and complaints became the baking soda to my vinegar, the perfect combination for an eruption. I've learned that if I explode, all I do is harm everyone around me, including myself. There is a better way. A more godly way. When I feel the unsaintly urge to lash out, I close my eyes. Breathe. Picture my Shepherd. He's here, right beside me. He gently leads those who have young—that's me. He beckons me to cast my burdens His way. He shows me the scars on His wrists that took all the sins away. He tenderly whispers that there is a way of escape from every temptation to explode. Instead, we can take the opportunity to grow in self-control and speak life.

PARENTING SCRIPT:

"Boys, I'm wondering who will have the biggest Jesus heart this morning?" I question them.

"I hear some arguing, and I care, but I bet one or both of you is going to be generous this morning," I challenge them.

"Go ahead and take a break if it's too hard to get along right now," I suggest.

"Son, it sounds like you have something on your mind that must be troubling you for you to talk like that to me. It's not who you really are. I'm here to listen whenever you are ready to share. In the meantime, please be respectful to me as I am being respectful to you," I caution him.

"Hey kiddos, it's the weekend and I have some fun things for us to do, but first we are going to have some restful time together here at home. I'm watching to see who tries to outdo one another with brotherly love. Can't wait to see who steps up and how you choose to be helpful!" I chirp.

I'm calm. I'm empathetic, even though I churn inside. We can do and say the right things until our emotions catch up. Moms and dads, it's Saturday. It may not be relaxing. But it is your life, and it's a good one because you are becoming stronger in your faith as you help shape theirs. Temporary peace on earth and angelic children will not afford you treasure in heaven, which is far more valuable. But, being willing to face the triggers and be refined into the image of Jesus brings with it incomparable riches.

However, **there's no way I will respond rightly when I'm empty spiritually**. Reading my Bible consistently has been my saving grace. As I wade through the emotional minefield of my child's drama, meditation on the truth makes all the difference in my responses. When I'm frustrated, whatever the day of the week, I keep these verses in mind:

there's no way I will respond rightly when I'm empty spiritually.

"He has told you, O man, what is good; and what does the Lord require of you but to do justice, and to love kindness, and to walk humbly with your God" (Micah 6:8)?

"And God is able to make all grace abound to you, so that having all sufficiency in all things at all times, you may abound in every good work" (2 Corinthians 9:8).

"Love one another with brotherly affection. Outdo one another in showing honor" (Romans 12:10).

"Love is patient and kind; love does not envy or boast; it is not arrogant or rude. It does not insist on its own way; it is not irritable or resentful; it does not rejoice at wrongdoing, but rejoices with the truth. Love bears all things, believes all things, hopes all things, endures all things" (I Corinthians 13:4-7).

"But hospitable, a lover of good, self-controlled, upright, holy, and disciplined" (Titus 1:8).

"Do not be overcome by evil, but overcome evil with good" (Romans 12:21).

Our children will behave childishly but it's up to us to pave the way to maturity. Our role as parents will be one we will most likely fulfill till the day God calls us home. Luke 9:23 says, "And he said to all, "If anyone would come after me, let him deny himself and take up his cross daily and follow me." If my daily life involves children, there is no day off from denying myself when it comes to being more like Jesus. No skip days from cross-bearing. There are no weekends in the spiritual realm. We might have had plans for a fun and happy Friday night, but God may have plans to refine us through the squabbles of our kids. Each day, we must yield our expectations to the Lord. Instead of a leisure day, we may wake up to a training day.

It's Saturday all right. And I'm busy over here being refined and taking the opportunity to point my kids to Christ.

Join me?

SCRIPT-URE:

"And God is able to make all grace abound to you, so that having all sufficiency in all things at all times, you may abound in every good work"

(2 Corinthians 9:8)

PRAYER SCRIPT:

"Oh Lord, I have room for improvement, I know. I often want my way instead of persevering through the challenges of parenting. Thank You for promising to help me in every moment of every day. It's hard when I desire peace and harmony, especially on a weekend, and instead, my kids make life unpleasant. But I know we are all on a journey toward being refined. Help me, Lord, to yield my desires to You so I will be strengthened to keep doing the good parenting, even when it's inconvenient. Bring peace to our home because we are eager to be like Christ and help us grow toward that end. Give us all a desire to outdo one another in honor and affection and give us a beautiful weekend. In Jesus' name, amen!

MAKE THE SCRIPT YOUR OWN:

What are your overall expectations for the weekend as a family? Have you gone out of your way to set your kids up for success by communicating with them, coaching them, and providing ways for them to meet your expectations? Is there room for collaboration? When everything goes wrong, what is the biblical way to make it right? What do your kids need to hear? In the workbook pages, write out your own script for weekend battles that fits your own family dynamics.

Chapter 19 —
When They're Never
Satisfied and Always
Pushing for More

Wendy

Your words matter. You know it's true, but you also know it's miserably hard to choose your words carefully in a moment of conflict. **When a child is doing wrong, it's hard to do right and speak right and speak life.** But we must. Proverbs 18:21 says, "The tongue has the power of life and death," so we must deliberately choose to speak life.

> *When a child is doing wrong, it's hard to do right and speak right and speak life.*

Even when their little love tanks never seem to get all filled up, and they're pushing for more when you're all emptied out—even then, moms and dads, even then, you need to keep doing and saying and loving *and parenting*. No one told me how it would feel to offer a cookie to a child and somehow have them argue with me for more rather than cheerfully accepting the gift with a smile and a thanks. No one told me how sad I'd feel shuffling out of my child's room at night because after all the lullabies and prayers, the child cried over not getting one more book. And because no one told me, because I didn't know, I didn't know I needed to have a plan of what to say and what to do. But I learned.

And every day I learn to apply this same old script to new scenarios.

PARENTING SCRIPT:

When my children are discontent and want more, we joyfully recount what they already have.

Not long ago, we were in the car on our way home from the fair with a cooler full of water bottles in the back. When the three started complaining because I refused to stop and get a milkshake, I used a variation of the script they've heard a hundred times before. "Hey you guys, I need everyone's attention." When their eyes were all fixed on my rear-view mirror I went on, "I have loved giving you all sorts of yeses today. Yes to the fair and yes to the Ferris wheel and yes to the petting zoo and yes to funnel cakes. But right now I'm giving you a no, and I need you to let your heart be all right with that. And I know you can be, after all, your heart is so full of all my other yeses today."

This is the heart and soul of my pre-planned script when discontentment grips their hearts and minds. When it's time for bed, but we didn't watch a movie, I remind them of all the yeses. And on those sacred Sundays when we choose to stay home after church rather than go exploring for more fun, I remind them of the sabbath, and the yeses we enjoy the other six days.

"Because your heart is so filled up by all of the other wonderful yeses you've been given, you're alright when the answer is no."

Do you see how easy it is to modify the particulars to meet the blessings of that day? Even today my oldest and I took my mom out for lunch. It wasn't just any ordinary lunch, it was the Cheesecake Factory for my mom's birthday, and we shared a slice of Godiva Cheesecake with her! Afterwards we walked by shops with trendy hats and tee shirts, but we didn't have the time or the budget to stop. All I said, quietly in his ear was, "Can you tell me all of the yeses you already got today?"

Use this script enough and your children will be able to answer the question on their own after a while. And isn't that the goal? In one of the early chapters I encouraged you to soothe your crying child in a way that teaches him to eventually be a big kid with self-soothing skills. Our goals aren't just for today, but for tomorrow too. The same is true here: we walk them through their blessings so they have the skill to do the same on their own one day, because contentment is a character trait that doesn't come naturally for most in this day and age. **Contentment must be learned, and we're the ones to teach it.**

"I know what it is to be in need, and I know what it is to have plenty. I have learned the secret of being content in any and every situation, whether well fed or hungry, whether living in plenty or in want. I can do all this through him who gives me strength" (Philippians 4:12-13, NIV).

"Keep your lives free from the love of money and be content with what you have, because God has said, 'Never will I leave you; never will I forsake you'" (Hebrews 13:5, NIV).

"But godliness with contentment is great gain. For we brought nothing into the world, and we can take nothing out of it" (1 Timothy 6:6-7, NIV).

"Then he said to them, 'Watch out! Be on your guard against all kinds of greed; life does not consist in an abundance of possessions'" (Luke 12:15, NIV).

There's a list of Bible verses a mile long we could add to this chapter, and I do encourage you to do a study on biblical contentment if this is a struggle for you and your kids. However, be careful not to berate your children with the help of Scripture. We want them to love God's Word and find encouragement there. As we suggest in all of these chapters, don't lecture them in your anger (and certainly not with the help of Scripture), but find a time to figure out what you truly mean to say, and then apply it like medicine with the help of the Great Physician. That's the cure.

In a moment of contentment, affirm their thankful hearts and open up the Word of God together. Look up the verses above, then ask your kids to worship the Lord by recounting to Him (not you) all of the yeses they've already had that day.

"Thank You for the bacon we had for breakfast. And for our mom who fried it up. And our trip to Grandma's. And thank You for the grapes You made, the ones that taste just like cotton candy! And thank You for mini-figures and boogie boards too. And playdates, thank You for playdates."

The key to my success with this script is how consistently I can use it—because we still need it daily. Contentment is a slow-growing fruit for many of us. I'm tempted every now and again to blame them and shame them for their entitled fits, but the truth is their dad and I struggle with contentment too! But the more often I say this script, the more often we're all reminded to focus on the blessings we already have.

SCRIPT-URE:

"But godliness with contentment is great gain. For we brought nothing into the world, and we can take nothing out of it"
(1 Timothy 6:6-7, NIV)

PRAYER SCRIPT:

Dear God, You have given us everything we need for life and godliness (2 Peter 1:3). Every good and perfect gift comes from You (James 1:17). You take care of the birds of the air (Matthew 6:26) and the beasts of the fields (Psalm 147:9). How much more will You provide for us? And so I trust You when we've got a lot or when we've got a little. (Philippians 4:11) I do trust You, and I'm thankful ... but I want to trust You more and be even more thankful. I want to be content with what we have. And I want our children to learn to be grateful and content as well. Teach me first, Lord, so I can model a content heart for the kids you've given me. In Jesus' name, amen.

MAKE THE SCRIPT YOUR OWN:

Do you struggle with discontentment yourself? Is this a generational pattern you see flaring up? Which of the verses above about contentment would be the best one for you to hide in your heart today and then pass onto them in moments void of conflict? Write it out in the workbook pages, and consider what times your children struggle most with contentment and how you might address it the next time they do.

Chapter 20 — When Your Child Needs To Handle Disappointment

Amber

Is there a life skill you wish you had mastered before life hit you squarely between the eyes? As an adult, there are a few lessons I wish I had learned as a child that could have saved me a lot of heartache. I often think about my struggle with handling disappointment as a child. Grappling with loss was not my strength. To this day it is still a challenge. Many of us had parents who fell into one of two camps. One camp told us to stop sniveling and suck it up when we faced disappointment. We stuffed our emotions and dried our tears, but the confusion and pain remained. The other camp wooed and coddled us in an attempt to shield us from any disappointment at all, giving in to us if we protested anything or everything. We never learned to cope and became adults who often view the world with a victim mentality. Neither camp made us happy campers in the end because we grew up without the life skills to manage our emotions in a biblical way. Some of us walked away from God entirely, distrusting His ability to help us in our time of need.

Personally, when my children's reactions to disappointment are unreasonable, I can quickly become unreasonable too. On a scale of one to ten, their problem may be a three, but their reaction is a ten! So my reaction to their reaction registers a twelve! Does this sound familiar? You provide your daughter a day full of fun, allowing her to sit beside you while you both get a pedicure, but she dissolves into a tantrum when you say no to going through the drive through on your way home for lunch. Your son slams his bedroom door in anger because you won't let his friend come over, even though you made his favorite breakfast and he has a fun night ahead at a baseball game to look forward to. We say to ourselves, "How can she be so ungrateful? After all I do for her?" Or, "What a selfish boy I have! Who does he think he is?" Instead of asking these kinds of defensive questions and allowing negative thinking to derail good parenting, a more productive approach is just one script away.

PARENTING SCRIPT:

I asked my son, Oliver, this question the other day when he was battling disappointment. "What can you do when things are not going the way you want them to?" His answer caught me happily off guard, "Trust God." And of course he's one hundred percent right. I went on to affirm him, offering this tried and true reminder:

"When you are feeling down, look up!"

He lifted his sorrowful gaze to meet my empathetic eyes. "When we look up to God, He can lift our spirits. It's an act of trusting Him and His plan for us when people or circumstances disappoint us. It's okay to feel sad, but we should allow our sorrows to drive us closer to the Lord." He nodded, able to move on to the next part of our day with a renewed spirit.

The very next afternoon we had occasion to rehearse the script again, "When you are feeling down, look up!" Sometimes, "looking up" means a simple prayer where we honestly express our hurt, asking God to heal our hearts, placing our faith in the One we cannot see but in Whom we believe. That's exactly what Oliver and I did. And that's exactly the kind of holy habit that will equip him for the future.

This generation needs to be girded with the truth that emotions are God-given and healthy, but they do not rule the heart and mind of a son or daughter of God. That's the job of the Holy Spirit. As a young adult, my disappointments nearly crushed me. **I never want my children to believe that their circumstances have more power over their lives than their God.** Jeremiah 29:11 is a promise revealing the heart of the Lord for His people: "For I know the plans I have for you, declares the Lord, plans for welfare and not for evil, to give you a future and a hope." If our kids find a godly balance between suffering and hope in their youth, nothing will stop them from fulfilling God's will for them when they are grown. Nor will they allow discouragement to defeat them.

> *I never want my children to believe that their circumstances have more power over their lives than their God.*

Author Kay Arthur says, "The disappointment has come—not because God desires to hurt you or make you miserable or to demoralize you or ruin your life or keep you from ever knowing happiness. He wants you to be perfect and complete in every aspect, lacking nothing. It's not the easy times that make you more like Jesus but the hard times." When we misunderstand the purpose of how God may be using disappointment in our lives, life becomes a series of problems that wound us instead of obstacles permitted to transform us. Our misfortunes give us the impression that we are overlooked or forgotten by God. Or worse, that He is not the good God we thought He was. What young person, when they are old enough to think for themselves, will walk with a God like that? *Not a one.* It's imperative that as we teach our kids to view setbacks through the lofty lens of Scripture, that they never view a heavenly God through a human microscope. Matthew 10: 29-31 affirms God's care for us: "Are not two sparrows sold for a penny? And not one of them will fall to the ground apart from your Father. But even the hairs of your head are all numbered. Fear not, therefore; you are of more value than many sparrows."

It's not uncommon for me to place my hand on my son's head in moments like these. I stroke his hair, and I tell him how hard it would be for me to count each strand. I remind him, as doubt fueled by disappointment swirls in his mind, that God knows the number of every golden hair tucked behind his ear. We don't want to be the parent who doesn't have time for this. We never want to dismiss our child's sorrow, immature though it may be. Nor do we want to value peace and quiet so much that we settle for the easy yes to placate our children. Instead, let us wade through discouragement together. Let us, and our children, place our trust in God in whom we will never be disappointed.

SCRIPT-URE:

"Are not two sparrows sold for a penny? And not one of them will fall to the ground apart from your Father. But even the hairs of your head are all numbered. Fear not, therefore; you are of more value than many sparrows"

(Matthew 10: 29-31)

PRAYER SCRIPT:

Lord, thank You for loving me and my children with a love we can't even begin to comprehend. Nothing happens to us without Your permission. Father, You have good plans for us that include heaven as our future. We do not have to wallow in our temporary disappointments in this life. Allow me to teach my children to place their hope in You, not in people, positions, or possessions. Heal our broken hearts, give us hope, and help us to keep our eyes fixed on You! Thank You, Lord, for caring about the things we care about, but also caring enough not to leave us in our sad state. In Jesus' name, amen!

MAKE THE SCRIPT YOUR OWN:

How do you handle disappointment? Is your view of God based on what the Bible says or on your feelings? What's your typical response when your child displays an unreasonable reaction to loss? In the workbook pages, write out your own script for managing disappointment that fits your own family dynamics.

Chapter 21 — When Lecturing Doesn't Work (AKA - Silent Scripts)

Wendy

I stepped down from the platform and walked toward the back of the room. The ladies all around me were launching into the discussion questions I'd planned for them, except one young mom who was making a beeline straight for me. Without a formal introduction she blurted out in desperation:

"My four year old doesn't respect my authority at all. She sees herself as my equal and constantly speaks hatefully and disrespectfully. I end up lecturing her whenever it happens, but nothing changes. It's so hard. I don't have any control because she thinks that she's in control! And the more I talk the less she listens!"

Before I could invite her to sit with me and talk it through, she continued on, standing in the middle of the room, with a dozen large tables all around us. "Just this morning when we were getting in the car to come here, she was trying to climb from the back of the car into my front seat. I wasn't mad, I wasn't mean, I simply put my arm out to stop her, and she says, 'Mom! You're pushing me! Stop pushing me!' When I said that I did not push her and her tone was not honoring, she yelled, 'No! You did push me, and you're talking mean to me!' Even when I managed to get her strapped into her car seat, she argued with me all the way here. The childcare workers could not have taken her from me fast enough! What's more, this is totally normal for her. I have no idea what to do."

When she was done, she bowed her head, and a few tears fell straight from her eyes to the floor. They didn't even roll down her cheeks—they just dropped and splashed at our feet.

"I'm glad you're here," I said sincerely, then hugged her a long time.

"Oh, you don't want to hug me," she whimpered, "My daughter and I just got over lice."

"That just makes me want to hug you extra-long." And I did.

When we were knee to knee at an empty table in the back of the room, I asked her, "What would have happened had you not come this morning? What if you had simply stopped the car and stopped talking?"

She looked up with a wet face, "What? But that's punishing me not her! We missed the last two weeks because ..." she scratched her head and made a ridiculous face. It was too pathetic not to laugh, so we did.

"I know," I said with sincerity, "That makes sense. However, what if each and every time she was rude and disrespectful, you stopped everything and said nothing? Four years old is old enough, and she sounds like she's smart. It wouldn't take her long to learn that you're the one in charge. What would you be willing to give up *today* to teach her a lesson that could last all her tomorrows? She doesn't hear your words. When she does wrong, she doesn't hear your words."

"If I'd taken her out of the car and brought her straight back into the house this morning, she would have ..." again the mom started to pantomime and make a crazy face.

I filled in the blanks, "'But Mommy,' she probably would have cried, 'all my friends are going to be there and you said we could go to Chick-fil-A with Ansley and her mom afterward. You liiiiiiied.'"

She nodded and laughed a sad laugh, because I perfectly nailed how the conversation would have gone. "What if instead of lecturing her on your way, you had simply stopped? Stopped the car. Stopped your lecture. Stopped the fun."

"She makes me so angry!" She said it wide eyed.

"Your anger isn't the problem. Reacting in anger may be your problem, but feeling it isn't. I started to sweat and even tremble just hearing your story. Psalm 4:4 is one of my favorite verses for parents when they're angry, because it affirms the emotion of anger. It says, 'Be angry, and do not sin; ponder in your own hearts on your beds, and be silent. Selah.' The NIV translation may be even better for parents of four year olds, because it says, 'Tremble, and do not sin; Meditate in your heart upon your bed, and be still. Selah.' Have you ever gotten so mad you started to tremble?"

I love this verse because it gives us permission:

1. to be angry

2. to be silent

3. to talk it through with God, not our kids.

"Be angry, and do not sin; ponder in your own hearts on your beds, and be silent. Selah" (Psalm 4:4).

When our children do wrong, it is ok to feel angry and to give yourself a parental-time-out to talk it through with God. Our kids know how to tune us out sometimes, but He never does. He's always listening, always cares, and always has the answer we're looking for.

Feel all the feelings that you feel, but don't sin. Instead sit quietly and talk it through with Him. Meditate in your heart. Moms and dads tend to miss this step. They go straight from the command to not sin and try to muscle through correction without anger. What if instead we just got really still and really silent? This isn't the same thing as giving our loved ones the silent treatment, by the way. *Most kids know what's wrong when they've done wrong ... so be quiet.* This is treating them lovingly by using no words, rather than manipulating them with your silence and making them guess what's wrong. **Most kids know what's wrong when they've done wrong ... so be quiet.**

In other chapters I've suggested being quiet as you figure out what it is you truly want to say. But this chapter is different, because sometimes you need to simply remain silent ... totally and completely.

Maybe your words have lost their power, and you need a silent script that has the power to communicate a crystal clear message when your children are throwing a belligerent fit, when they are doing what they know is wrong, when they're disrespecting you *and they know better.*

Here are a few of my favorite "Silent Scripts" that help me to speak loud and clear without saying a word.

SILENT SCRIPTS:

Stop.

When they are doing and saying something blatantly awful, you don't need to respond in like. Just stop and wait, then wait some more if need be. This silent script has more power than any string of words ever strung together in anger.

Raise your hand.

When they're going on and on, but you don't need to hear another word, raise your hand. **Raise your hand, don't raise your voice.** It's amazing how quickly your child will remember their preschool days and quiet their lips.

Pull the car over.

Are you running late? Perhaps. Is it inconvenient? Absolutely. But before you lose your business and throw a fit to match theirs, pull the car over. When I'm really struggling to stay in control of myself, I've even learned to get out of the car for a moment to pray. I don't mean that I leave them there for a long stretch, just long enough for me to regain my own composure. If they try to follow you out, refer back to the last silent script and raise your hand. They will stay buckled in.

With all of these silent scripts, I'm always amazed how much more power I have when I don't speak than when I lecture and nag. And there are *so many* Bible verses that affirm being quiet rather than lecturing and shaming.

"The one who has knowledge uses words with restraint, and whoever has understanding is even-tempered. Even fools are thought wise if they keep silent, and discerning if they hold their tongues" (Proverbs 17:27-28, NIV).

"Therefore at such a time the prudent person keeps silent, for it is an evil time" (Amos 5:13).

"My dear brothers and sisters, take note of this: Everyone should be quick to listen, slow to speak and slow to become angry" (James 1:19, NIV).

"For thus the Lord GOD, the Holy One of Israel, has said, 'In repentance and rest you will be saved, In quietness and trust is your strength.' But you were not willing'"(Isaiah 30:15).

"Surely I have composed and quieted my soul; Like a weaned child rests against his mother, My soul is like a weaned child within me" (Psalm 131:2).

"Make it your ambition to lead a quiet life and attend to your own business and work with your hands, just as we commanded you" (1 Thessalonians 4:11).

Hiding these Scriptures in your heart will you help you when you're tempted to sin against your children because they've sinned against you.

SCRIPT-URE:

"Tremble, and do not sin; Meditate in your heart upon your bed, and be still. Selah"

(Psalm 4:4)

PRAYER SCRIPT:

Dear Lord, Your Word is like a burning coal that touches my lips and cauterizes the flow of unnecessary words. The more I ingest Your commandments, the more my words become laced with Your Word and Your love. And I am grateful. Therefore, I invite You, Lord, to show me when to speak and when to be silent and how to be silent with grace and love. You've told me that quietness and trust is my strength (Isaiah 30:15). I'm willing to learn to be quiet and trust You more, even when I'd rather roll steadily along, lecturing everyone in my path. Help me Lord to speak as You speak and be silent when You would have me to speak without words. In Jesus' name I humbly ask, amen.

MAKE THE SCRIPT YOUR OWN:

When are you most inclined to lecture on and on? Do your words fall on deaf ears and stony hearts? Perhaps it's in the evening when you're in the kitchen making dinner. You've asked them to hold off on any more snacks, but they throw fits and yell and go into the pantry anyway. Or maybe they get belligerent with you on Saturday mornings when they don't understand why they can't go where they want to go. I wish we could sit face-to-face, like I did with that exasperated mom that day, and brainstorm through the hardest times to plan some silent scripts together. In the workbook pages, I encourage you to do that now.

Chapter 22 —
When Their Tone of Voice
Is Angry, Rude, or Whiny

Amber

Charles R. Swindoll said, "Life is 10% what happens to you and 90% how you react to it." It rings true from my wavy-haired head to my neon painted toenails. The only portion of this thought that gives me pause is that word "react." In our book, *Triggers: Exchanging Parents' Angry Reactions for Gentle Biblical Responses*, I discuss the need for parents to learn to *respond* to kids instead of *reacting* to them. Reacting sounds helpless and impulsive. It's what we do when we feel offended and angry. Responding is thoughtful, self-controlled, and intentional. It's what we do when we see a negative situation as an opportunity for growth, refinement, and blessing. And that's exactly what every trigger is.

It's all well and good to imagine ourselves responding to our kids instead of reacting. It's another to do it. Reality often looks more like a boxing match where words fly between siblings and parents with all the force of an uppercut to the jaw. Child one enters the scene, blubbering heatedly because her brother took the shiny new bike from her. Child two is hot on her heels, screeching, "Noooo, that's not true! It was my turn anyway!" The noise level of both children reverberates through the chambers of your assaulted brain and you can't even begin to address them for all the competing expressions of anger, whining, and complaining. Before you can stutter one word out of your frazzled brain, child one has a handful of child two's hair and shoves her to the ground. You thought you were a parent, not a referee at a qualifying round for World Wrestling Entertainment.

It's a chain of reactions. Your son reacts to your daughter for not letting him have his turn on the big bike. Your daughter reacts to him by fighting back. You react in frozen disbelief and confusion. She reacts by grabbing a fist full of curly hair. He reacts by laying his hands on her. One dreadful domino after another, leading to a crescendo of turmoil. Now it's your turn. *To react or not to react?* While less poetic than Shake-speare's "To be or not to be?," it's the defining question every parent faces a hundred times a day.

Responding to the circumstances and kids in our lives is entirely different than reacting. At it its core, responding happens when we stop being surprised by childishness, immaturity, and sinfulness. Being flabbergasted by whiny toddlers and rude teenagers disables us. Being prepared to see these moments as opportunities to model appropriate responses to one another by our own right responses is stewardship at its best. As Wendy often reminds us, we aren't victims, helpless to know what to do. We are moms and dads who are empowered by the Holy Spirit to bless instead of curse, to offer loving consequences and gentle corrections, choosing to walk our talk.

If we don't show them what is right and good in word and deed, then who will? If not in the middle of the conflict as the heat of temptation creeps up our necks, then when? Knowing what we can say in these moments takes us from reacting to responding and from harassed to hopeful. The right script isn't crafted on the fly—it's designed for times such as these.

PARENTING SCRIPT:

When any child of mine whines, complains, is rude, or uses their tone of voice as a weapon in any way, this is the script that stops them in their tracks and allows me to respond in gentleness:

"Son, how can you say that differently?"

As soon as the words are out of my mouth, their entire demeanor softens. They transition from perturbed to pliable. My kids are so used to me using this script by now that one question is all it takes for them to immediately "try again," another phrase I offer when they forget who they are talking to. I don't say that with a sway of my hips and a finger wag like I'm the boss and you better not disrespect me. No, it's a "try that again" with a calm, loving, yet authoritative tone. They aren't talking to someone who will let rude or mean words escape. They are talking to a mom or dad who loves them and is willing to coach them toward communicating rightly.

Sometimes, the turmoil within them is so muddled that they carry on with wrong words and an ugly tone. It's then that I say:

"Let's take a break to cool down. When you can come and talk to me in a calm and normal voice, I will be happy to listen to you. Then we can sort out what you need. I want to help, but I simply can't help you when you speak to me like that."

If our words tumble out from our flesh, they will be deadly and full of ruin. Words that bring life flow from a heart and

We can't speak the truth in love if there is no truth or love to draw from.

mind that is committed to abiding in Christ. **We can't speak the truth in love if there is no truth or love to draw from.** Meditating on Scripture is the place to begin. Some of these verses bear repeating:

"Let no corrupting talk come out of your mouths, but only such as is good for building up, as fits the occasion, that it may give grace to those who hear" (Ephesians 4:29).

"A soft answer turns away wrath, but a harsh word stirs up anger" (Proverbs 15:1).

"If anyone thinks he is religious and does not bridle his tongue but deceives his heart, this person's religion is worthless" (James 1:26).

"For those who live according to the flesh set their minds on the things of the flesh, but those who live according to the Spirit set their minds on the things of the Spirit" (Romans 8:5).

Besides my own devotion to believing the Word of God and trusting the Lord to influence me so I can influence my kids, the one thing that has helped me train my boys the most is my *consistency*. It's a theme Wendy and I weave throughout all our books together. If I want to teach them to speak to me with loving kindness and respect, then I need to treat them the way I want to be treated as God encourages us to do in Luke 6:31. I also need to respect myself enough to not permit them to speak in a way that dishonors me or others. Give in to whining, angry outbursts, and rudeness, and you will get a whole lot more of it. Still, we can address their sin without adding ours into the mix. As much as we want to be consistent in our parenting, may we be even more consistent in our modeling.

Be open to this next question. What have you been allowing them to get away with? Take those moments as opportunities to retrain their tongues, and you will begin to partner with God to open their hearts to Holy Spirit transformation. The family setting is our children's training ground. Parents who enter the arena ignorant that their home is the ring where spiritual battles are lost or won will often feel bruised and battered at the end of every day. Is that how you feel? Wounded by your child's words? Is it a losing battle in your home? Do you come away from interactions with your child more defeated than delighted? Let me encourage you. The training won't end, but the tug-of-war can.

Your teenager grunts when you ask for his help. He retorts with a sarcastic, "No thanks."

"I don't think that's how you meant to say that, Son. Why don't you pause a moment and try again?" you recommend.

He may very well stay put, ignoring you, showing you he thinks your home is one where members don't help one another. Every man is for himself. Later that day, the natural consequence is his surprise when he finds out that the dinner table is one plate short—at his seat. His favorite meal steams from the other dishes as he sits bewildered:

"Where's mine?" he complains.

"I thought you wanted to live in a house where you and I don't serve and help one another," you say, kindly. It seemed that was how you wanted it when I asked for help earlier. I guessed you wouldn't mind then if I didn't help you out by setting a place for you. I'll go ahead and get you a plate this time then. And I'll expect the same from you too, when I ask for help next time. Gently, you remind him, "In this family, we reflect the heart of Jesus by loving and serving one another. That's what we do. It's better that way, don't you think?" You smile with sincerity, loving him enough to show him the way with dignity and grace instead of angry reactions.

He knows you're *for him*. Coaching him to not just win the round, but to take hold of the championship prize—a title worth training for today and tomorrow. He needs a coach who knows what to say and how to say it to get him there. That's you. That's me. Responding not reacting. Parents who enter the ring, ready to coach, towel slung around their shoulders and water bottles ready, prepared to cheer and guide their child toward victory, who go to bed at night equally exhausted *but never drained*. They rest easy, ready for another day to fight the spiritual battle for their home. They are tired but eager, ready to go another round.

SCRIPT-URE:

"A soft answer turns away wrath, but a harsh word stirs up anger"

(Proverbs 15:1)

PRAYER SCRIPT:

Father, You are good. Thank You for loving my children and me even when we speak rudely, whine, and complain. You love us too much to let us continue in our sinful ways. Cleanse our mouths by cleansing our hearts. Help me to stop and think very carefully about responding to my child instead of reacting to him/her. Work in my son's/daughter's heart as well, so they will learn to speak to me with respect, kindness, and love. Let them see me model this consistently in my life too. Lord, let us become a family who honors one another above ourselves. Let us build one another up as we grow in maturity, and give us all grace for one another when we fall short. In Jesus' name, amen!

MAKE THE SCRIPT YOUR OWN:

What does your child struggle with the most when it comes to tone of voice? Do you usually react or respond? What's one thing you can change in your body language to respond instead of react? In the workbook pages, write out your own script for responding with respect that fits your own family dynamics.

Chapter 23 —
When Children Tattle

Wendy

Two little girls ran up the stairs crying over what the big kids had said and done. "They're mean and we won't ever play with them again!" We were vacationing with some of our dearest friends, and the children had been getting along great! But three days into our adventures, and the novelty was wearing off.

"What did the big kids do?" I asked with sincere tenderness as I wiped away their tears. Their mom was in the other room and let me handle the trouble.

"They said we couldn't keep changing the rules for the game they were playing, but their rules were dumb, and we kept losing! They were mean, and they yelled. So we knocked it over and yelled back, and then they threw our stuffed animals out of the room and told us to get out!" Again with the tears.

"Would you like for me to tell you what I tell my own kids when we're home? It's also what I'll go down there and tell them in just a few minutes. Do you want to know what I'm going to say?"

"Yes," they said in Dolby sound.

PARENTING SCRIPT:

"There's only one person you can control."

The twins looked at me confused. But had my boys been there, that's all the script they would have needed.

I went on, "I have no doubt that the big kids were unkind to you …"

"They were awful and you've got to punish them! And we won't ever play with them again. No we won't." Again the girls cried and again the tears flowed. I held my hand in the air, just as I do at home for my own boys (remember, it's one of my favorite "Silent Scripts") The girls got real quiet.

"I have no doubt that the big kids were unkind to you," I repeated, "but you can't make them kind. You can only make you kind. In this life people will be unkind to you, but you can't control them. The only person God gave you any power over is you. Does that make sense?"

"Yes," one said, "but are you going to punish them?"

I laughed and said, "That's not your business. Your business is you. So why don't you tell me the things you did wrong?

"We threw their game and yelled at them," confessed one of the identical darlings.

"A lot," whispered the other.

"And that wasn't nice, was it?"

They both shook their heads quietly.

"I'm going to go talk to them about them, but before I do, would you like to be the biggest of the kids and tell them that you're sorry for what you did wrong?" Their eyes grew wide!

"That doesn't mean it was all your fault, but it means you recognize that what you did was wrong. And that's what big kids do. You control you."

The girls went down and apologized, then quickly came back. After dinner, I gave the same script to the big kids who wanted to focus on everything the six year olds had done wrong.

"There's only one person God gave you the power to control and that's yourself. **You do you.**"

While we would all love for our children to be fully mature today, they're not there yet. And honestly, neither are we. There's a holy order to growing up in Christ, and there's an order to our children growing up, too. It's not as elusive as it seems most days. It's actually quite simple. First we disciple our kids with words, then we discipline them with consequences, and finally they grow to be self-disciplined.

The tendency for most of us, however, is to start and end with the rod of discipline, and we wield it inconsistently. But **inconsistent discipline, without consistent discipleship, lacks power.** Discipline needs the foundation of discipleship to stand upon.

Disciple - Discipline - Self-Discipline

Here's what I mean: When my first-born was a toddler and his baby brother napped in a bassinet nearby, we would draw together, talk together, read together, be together. We memorized Scripture songs and prayed for our loved ones. We filled sticker books, laid out the tracks for Thomas the Tank Engine, and made cookies for neighbors. And in everything we did, every time we sat down, each naptime as we laid down and rose up again, I discipled my child.

"Hear, O Israel! The Lord is our God, the Lord is one! You shall love the Lord your God with all your heart and with all your soul and with all your might. These words, which I am commanding you today, shall be on your heart. You shall teach them diligently to your sons and shall talk of them when you sit in your house and when you walk by the way and when you lie down and when you rise up. You shall bind them as a sign on your hand and they shall be as frontals on your forehead. You shall write them on the doorposts of your house and on your gates" (Deuteronomy 6:4-9).

Disciple

Our children are our dearest disciples. They follow our example, parrot our words, copy our expressions, and learn of our family values. We speak tenderly into their lives as they drift off to sleep and remind them what is true with gentle tones when they do what is wrong. During the years when they are young, every lesson requires us to get down on their level and look into their eyes. This is discipleship. We must remember we are raising disciples—our disciples when they are young, but God's disciples when the Holy Spirit calls them to a mature faith.

Discipline

As the years went by and my eldest son began playing with his baby brother and this mama swelled with a third little boy, my child began purposefully testing the waters of right and wrong. He defiantly exclaimed, "No!" Where there had once been compliance, I now found a strong will, iron fists, and determined glares. Though my natural reaction was to fight back, especially with pregnancy hormones heightening all of my emotions, I learned I could not let my son's recent transformation change me. My job was still the same: to parent him well.

The key is remembering that disobedience is a natural part of their growing up process. Finding where the boundaries lie, where their power lies, where mom and dad's lies too is all part of their job. **They push to find themselves, but we must not push back in anger or we might lose ourselves.**

They push to find themselves, but we must not push back in anger or we might lose ourselves

This season of willful disobedience heralds the start of our next parenting stage. This is when discipleship transitions to grace-based discipline. We love them, and so it is with the same gentle strength we remind them of what they already know to be true. Whether you use natural consequences or time-out chairs, the point is that there is a time and a place for discipline. And that time and place comes after you have already begun discipling them.

If discipleship is teaching a little person right from wrong, then discipline is reminding them what they already know is true. They have to know what's right before we can start disciplining them for doing wrong. Doesn't it seem backwards to discipline a toddler for doing something wrong if it's never been talked about? Discipleship is talking about it when they lie down and rise up and walk along the way with us.

Self-Discipline

With consistency, a day will come when we won't need to discipline them any more. They will have learned self-discipline. They will have learned how to turn the video game off and get to work without you nagging or threatening. They will have learned to get up in the morning and pack their bag for school, to call when they're running late, and ask for forgiveness when they've done wrong.

This is the natural progression of growing up. And it's how the Father grows us up, too. Walking with us and talking with us through His ever-present Holy Spirit, then teaching us through natural consequences when we've been willful. Eventually we grow up to bear the fruit of self-control, of self-discipline.

I am so thankful for the gentle way God has continued to grow me up, to disciple me with His near and abiding Spirit and through His living Word, to discipline and refine me through natural consequences, that I might walk in self-disciplined maturity. Let's follow His parental example as we purposefully parent our own children.

In the story at the beginning of this chapter I shared a script that I use in discipling my children. They need to know the only person God gave them the power to control is themselves! (The same is true for us, by the way.) The girls heard that message for the first time. Since my boys had heard it a hundred times before, I layered in some discipline. They put their game away, did the dishes after dinner, and played a different game with the little girls before bed.

"**You do you.**" They know what it means.

SCRIPT-URE:

"Hear, O Israel! The Lord is our God, the Lord is one! You shall love the Lord your God with all your heart and with all your soul and with all your might. These words, which I am commanding you today, shall be on your heart. You shall teach them diligently to your sons and shall talk of them when you sit in your house and when you walk by the way and when you lie down and when you rise up. You shall bind them as a sign on your hand and they shall be as frontals on your forehead.

You shall write them on the doorposts of your house and on your gates

(Deuteronomy 6:4-9)

PRAYER SCRIPT:

Dear Lord, thank You for never giving up on me. You are consistently gracious and kind, always speaking truth into my life through Your living Word and Your abiding Spirit. Teach me, Lord, to be more like You in the way I parent. I want to disciple my children, so one day they are Your disciples. I want to disciple them to know right from wrong as we walk together and talk together. From that loving place I will discipline them gently when they've chosen to do wrong. And from there, I know that with Your help, they can make the choice to be self-disciplined. That's the goal. Help them, Lord. And help me, I pray in Jesus' name, amen.

MAKE THE SCRIPT YOUR OWN:

Do your children come to you in the middle of a fight, when someone's hurt them and they've hurt that someone back? Would this script work then? "I don't doubt that your sister's done wrong, but people are going to hurt you in this life. How do you want to respond? God only gave you one person you can control. That's you. So you do you." In the workbook pages, pinpoint one of the areas where your kids tattle on each other most of all, and pen a script that encourages them to keep their eyes steady on their own behavior.

Chapter 24 —
When They Need
To Forgive One Another

Amber

Recently, I observed a squabble between two students on a field trip. There they stood, facing one another as the teacher urged them to apologize. One hung his head in sadness. The other glared stubbornly off into the distance, arms crossed in defiance.

"Sorry!" the offender eventually spat. His coerced apology fell flat on the victim. The teacher seemed satisfied enough, but there was no fooling the two children. One wasn't sorry, and the other wasn't relieved. They went away as troubled as when they came together. The only conscience cleared was the teacher's, who believed that as long as the rote response was voiced, his job was done.

In our home, the need for forgiveness is as common as mealtimes. The cycle of offense and forgiveness is one we rotate through regularly, whether between siblings or parents. I want my kids to apologize when they have wronged someone, but not at the cost of cheapening contrition. **Do we want meaningless apologies that devalue our relationships or sincere**

Do we want meaningless apologies that devalue our relationships or sincere repentance that enhances them?

repentance that enhances them? When it comes to forgiveness in our house, I'm not satisfied with empty externals. I want our relationships to be stronger in the aftermath of our struggles.

Very few aspects of growth in the Christian walk come easily. It'd be much easier to bury our heads in the sand and let kids fend for themselves, hoping for the best, or justify our growing resentment as we try to force pleasantries. But God calls us to a different approach. Forgiveness is not an option for the believer. The Bible is full of truths about the topic. Here are a handful of them:

"Be kind to one another, tenderhearted, forgiving one another, as God in Christ forgave you" (Ephesians 4:32).
"Then Peter came up and said to him, 'Lord, how often will my brother sin against me, and I forgive him? As many as seven times?' Jesus said to him, 'I do not say to you seven times, but seventy times seven'" (Matthew 18:21-22).
"Bearing with one another and, if one has a complaint against another, forgiving each other; as the Lord has forgiven you, so you also must forgive" (Colossians 3:13).

"But I say to you who hear, Love your enemies, do good to those who hate you, bless those who curse you, pray for those who abuse you" (Luke 6:27-28).

Pastor and author, John Piper, says this about the subject:

"Here is forgiveness: when you feel that someone is your enemy or when you simply feel that you or someone you care about has been wronged, forgiveness means,

1. resisting revenge,

2. not returning evil for evil,

3. wishing them well,

4. grieving at their calamities,

5. praying for their welfare,

6. seeking reconciliation so far as it depends on you,

7. and coming to their aid in distress. (http://www.desiring-god.org/messages/as-we-forgive-our-debtors).”

The goal of an apology in every family should be to restore and bring healing through forgiveness. It is to make amends by mending that which has unraveled—the bond of trust, peaceful spirits, and righting wrongs. Being ready to apologize or forgive is not an automatic state of being in the aftermath of conflict. It can take time, but it is far better to allow for breathing room than forcing an insincere apology or sweeping problems under the rug. Sometimes, the guilty party is ready to ask for forgiveness, but the wounded sibling isn't quite available emotionally to offer it. In both cases, parents would do well to coach them toward harmonious reconciliation instead of a hasty reparation.

PARENTING SCRIPT:

After emotions have died down a bit, I go to one or the other of my children and say this:

“What do you need to do to repair or mend your relationship?”

Sometimes, with a sulking child, I simply say in passing:

“I know you are upset but I hope that at some point you will mend your relationship with your dad/brother/sister.”

I let them mull that over, praying that the Holy Spirit will prompt them and work in their hearts. Just today, one of my youngest kids had a terrible meltdown over pizza. Pretty ridiculous, right? Well, it wasn't ridiculous to him. And he let his father know it by messing up his bedroom and being disrespectful. My wonderful husband kept calm, giving our son space to simmer down before speaking to him about right responses and better ways to manage disappointment. As our little guy came around, playing with his Legos, I sidled up to him and gently planted the idea of mending his relationship with his dad. He immediately ran to his father, wrapped his arms around him and said those two little words we love to hear, "I'm sorry." He meant it. Instead of an angry glare, his face was softened and his eyes were full of longing. He tilted his head up, eager for his dad's embrace. This became a truly teachable moment. Only then was our son open to listening. As a result, they got to practice more appropriate ways to communicate in the future.

Once our hearts are in the right place, ready to apologize, we teach this method for apologizing to one another in our family:

1. **Choose your timing wisely.** Go to the person and tell them that you would like to apologize to them, and make sure they are ready to listen to you. (Some of us are more emotional than others and need a little time to calm down so we can be receptive to the apology.)

2. **Take ownership for your sinfulness**. Apologize without any explanation for what you did or reasoning behind your behavior except for the sin that it was. (Explanations are usually justifications for wrong behavior that are not true apologies. This leads to further disagreements.) Your goal should be to take ownership for your own part in the

argument or circumstance, not to focus on their behavior or sinfulness.

For example, "Sarah, I reacted badly to what you said to me, and I should not have raised my voice and called you a name. I'm sorry for losing my self-control and hurting your feelings. I love you. Will you please forgive me?"

It does not sound like this, "Sarah, when you called me a baby it really hurt me, and so I got angry and called you a name. I wouldn't have done that if you hadn't hurt me first, so I'm sorry that I called you a name but next time, don't be mean to me. I'm sorry this happened."

As you can see, the blame is still being placed on the other person instead of taking ownership for his or her own wrongdoing. This is not a sincere apology. Proverbs 17:9 puts it like this, "The one who forgives an offense seeks love, but whoever repeats a matter separates close friends."

3. **Do not expect to get an apology back.** We teach our children that we can only control and manage our own hearts through the Holy Spirit's help. Similar to Wendy's simple script in chapter 23, "You do you," we can't control anyone else's forgiving heart but our own. When we want to restore our relationships, we must apologize and pray that our sibling or spouse will be receptive to our apology and that the relationship will be restored, but we can't go into it counting on that to happen. Otherwise, we will become angry again instead of simply meeting our goal to make things right on our end. However, we do teach our children that if someone apologizes to you, the right thing to do is indeed to forgive them! We want them to be able to say, "Thank you for your apology. I love you and I forgive you." Often, this prompts a similar apology from the other person.

4. **Don't keep a record of wrongs.** God does not remember our sins nor does He keep a record of our wrongs. Psalm 103:10-12 says, "He does not treat us as our sins deserve or repay us according to our iniquities. For as high as the heavens are above the earth, so great is his love for those who fear him; as far as the east is from the west, so far has he removed our transgressions from us." After restoration, we don't revisit or talk about that particular situation as a way of lording issues over one another in the future. Forgiveness is complete, and our attitudes are optimistic and hopeful that we will overcome these sinful attitudes with the help of the Lord Jesus.

5. **Pray for your siblings or spouse.** If there is a pattern of sinfulness, committed prayer is in order. It's not a self-righteousness prayer, but a reflective one that seeks to go to battle in the spiritual realms for ourselves, our kids, and our spouses.

Honestly, it's embarrassing if our child wrongs another and they don't want to make it right. Just like that teacher, we want to force an apology so we can have peace in our home and peace of mind. However, we trade a real opportunity to shape their character for a false sense of resolution. We have to get comfortable with the discomfort of not having immediate closure.

Forgiven people are forgiving people. I'm convinced that the quality of a forgiving spirit is one of the ways we can raise kids to live counter-culturally, winning others to Christ. Moreover, if our children learn to both forgive and accept forgiveness, they become adults who navigate their faith walk unburdened by the weight of sin, free to live life to the fullest as God intended. There may be areas I look back on as a mom with regret, but I'm certain when it comes to not requiring my kids to fake it in the forgiveness department, I'll be unapologetic.

SCRIPT-URE:

"Bearing with one another and, if one has a complaint against another, forgiving each other; as the Lord has forgiven you, so you also must forgive"

(Colossians 3:13)

PRAYER SCRIPT:

Father God, thank You for forgiving me! I never want my kids to misunderstand what forgiveness looks like because I am coercing them toward empty apologies. Help me to model a repentant heart and teach them how to apologize biblically. I'm sorry if I have harbored any resentment toward my children and their actions. Help me to be a forgiving parent. Lord, give us all humble hearts, ready to show mercy and quick to forgive! May my children grow up to be free from the burden of guilt and may we all walk in the freedom of Your great love. In Jesus' name, amen!

MAKE THE SCRIPT YOUR OWN:

What is the most challenging aspect of forgiveness for you personally? How do you feel about giving kids room to sort through their feelings or take time to calm down before attempting reconciliation? Which of the steps for apologizing biblically might be the most challenging for your family? Which step brings you the most peace? In the workbook pages, write out your own script for apologizing biblically that fits your own family dynamics.

Chapter 25 —
What Do You Need to
Stop Saying to Your Kids?

Wendy

Sitting beside them during homework, sighing frazzled sighs, "Come on buddy, this one's easy!" At the breakfast table, harping on the slow child, "Every day! Every day you're the last one to the table. What's wrong with you?" Breaking up squabbles between siblings, with our arms and with our words, "Other families don't have these problems. Other kids know how to love each other better than this." Daily exasperated, "Your teacher sent me another email. Why can't you just stop talking?" Or worse, "Shut up!" Trying to catch a moment alone behind the bathroom door, only to be found out. They pound and talk at you when you need a private moment, and out the words fly, "Leave me alone!"

Sometimes we say things in our anger, other times in our exasperation, and still other times from a place of good intention—simply not understanding how our words are being received.

I think we all have words we'd like to stop saying, but out they soar like daggers unsheathed. However, we must keep our words in when they don't produce life. Though you may feel hopeless, we are not powerless. We have the ability, with the help of the Holy Spirit at work within us, to "take captive every thought to make it obedient to Christ" (2 Corinthians 10:5, NIV).

So here's my question: what are the words that need to be eradicated from your parental vocabulary? Why do you say them and where do they come from? I hope you'll be honest with yourself in the pages of this private book, so you can pinpoint which of your words tear down rather than build up, defeat rather than cheer them on to victory, bring death and not life.

Ann Voskamp once wrote, "Trust your tongue only when your heart is tender." Finding moments like this one now, void of conflict when your heart is tender, to consider the right response when our children's behavior is wrong is the main theme of this book. However, today I want to suggest something new. What if, instead of writing ourselves new scripts, we chose to forego some of them altogether? You know the old adage: "If you don't have anything nice to say, don't say anything at all."

Do you ever grow tired of hearing yourself speak? Have you taken to saying curse words at your loved ones because nothing else seems to penetrate? Perhaps your incessant harping doesn't need a new script, maybe you need to simply be quiet every now and again. Because, "Too much talk leads to sin. Be sensible and keep your mouth shut" (Proverbs 10:19, NLT).

Proverbs 21:23 promises us, "Whoever keeps his mouth and his tongue keeps himself out of trouble." Sometimes silence is the best answer to the problem. Of course, some of you were raised by parents who gave you the silent treatment when they were displeased. They might not have yelled, but goodness did their silence bring guilt and shame upon the entire family. That's not what I'm suggesting here. I'm simply saying it's okay to not correct every wrong action with an equally wrong reaction, especially if you can't think of life-giving words with which to respond in the moment.

If you have resorted to saying unkind words to your children, consider stopping your mouth all together!

> *"For our struggle is not against flesh and blood, but against the rulers, against the authorities, against the powers of this dark world and against the spiritual forces of evil in the heavenly realms" (Ephesians 6:12, NIV).*

We are not fighting against flesh and blood, and so we do not need to lash out against our flesh and blood. Parenting is a spiritual fight. Therefore, we must armor up and arm ourselves with spiritual weaponry. An arsenal of faith, a quiver of Scripture promises, and feet shod with the gospel of peace.

We are not fighting against flesh and blood, and so we do not need to lash out against our flesh and blood.

Christ is our example in life at all times, especially in this season. We need His example. Many of Christ's responses to those who came against Him were counter-intuitive. He was justified, as King of all creation, yet He did not sin. Don't you feel justified, as their parent, to hurl a curse word or two, or in the least a shaming blow or a good tongue-lashing? But Christ endured their sin all the way to the cross.

Again, I'm not suggesting we ignore sin in our homes, but that we still our tongues and consider grace before responding before blowing up and blowing it with our children. **Hold** it in, and hold it back, and hold your children, and hold your tongue, and consider a better response today.

PARENTING SCRIPT:

While I do believe silence is sometimes the most powerful script when we're tempted to react inappropriately, I have learned to RE-SCRIPT my negative words into positive responses, as Amber encouraged us to do in chapter 2. Let's keep building upon that foundation with a few more examples:

Your child doesn't come to the table for dinner, and you're tempted to say, "How come you never come when you're called?" (Which may be true, but it sets in stone who they are and how they "always" behave.) Try instead, "I know you are able to come to the table now."

When the child who lies does it again, instead of saying "You're always lying!" try, "Son, God made you a truth-teller, that's who you are!"

RESCRIPTING is just turning your negative blows into positive blessings!

Recently one reader sent me this example: When her college-aged son had done something dishonorable, instead of berating him she said, "I see you as an honorable man, son. I want to keep seeing you that way." Talk about turning that negative into a positive and a blow into a blessing!

When you're tempted to holler, "Shut up!" How about whispering, "I want to hear what you have to say, but now isn't the time. Save that story/question for after I put your sister down for her nap. Then I can listen. "Don't forget, there is death and life in the power of the tongue" (Proverbs 18:21).

When the children are talking nasty to one another and you want to join in with a nasty word or two, don't. Perhaps you're tempted to say, "You are the meanest to each other and I'm sick of it. I don't know why you're such jerks! Just go outside." How about trying, "You're *not* mean kids, but you sure are struggling to be nice. Why don't you spend some alone time in your rooms and then try again to be the sweet friends I know you are."

When my children were all toddlers, toddling at the park together, a friend of mine was correcting her oldest nearby. She'd been insensitive to her little brother, telling him harshly that she didn't want to play with him. The mother, my friend, could have corrected her with equal harshness. Instead, she used this simple script, "Give him hope honey, give your brother some hope." And without a moment's fuss, the sister said to the brother, "I'll play with you in five minutes!" And they all went on smiling. Amazing! "Give him some hope" must have been very familiar familial script in their home.

How might you rescript your arguments about school? When the child who struggles with schoolwork comes home with another low grade, having also forgotten to turn in the project he worked on all weekend, don't ask, "What's wrong with you?" Try this positive remark: "You have such a good mind. I know that it's hard to remember to turn things in. Your grades don't always show it, but I know you can learn well! I'm on your team. So take a break and have a snack while I make dinner, and I'll go through the schoolwork with you after dinner. I'm sure you'll understand it by the time we're through!"

Life or death, it's your choice. But making the right choice requires slowing down long enough to consider your words carefully.

SCRIPT-URE:

"My dear brothers and sisters, take note of this: Everyone should be quick to listen, slow to speak and slow to become angry, because human anger does not produce the righteousness that God desires"

(James 1:19-20)

I love verse twenty of this familiar scripture. Often times we quote James 1:19 and forget to include it, but it is so important. Righteousness is not the result of fast, harsh, knee-jerk reactions. As a matter of fact, God's Word tells us that out of a man's heart, his mouth speaks. Let us, therefore, slow down and allow Him to do some heart-work on us before we throw any more verbal swords at our kids.

PRAYER SCRIPT:

Dear Lord, thank You for convicting me today of the words I shouldn't say. Please don't leave me in this convicted place, but give me words of life to speak in their stead. Thank you for Your Word. You speak to me so gently and with such grace, verse by verse. Teach me by Your example to do the same in our home each day. As I learn to re-script my words, give me the power to hold my tongue and honor You. In Jesus' name I pray, amen.

MAKE THE SCRIPT YOUR OWN:

What are some of the words you hear yourself speaking that need to be re-scripted or thrown out altogether? You can! You can write yourself a better response—a more gentle response, a more gracious response, a more compassionate and understanding response that propels your children toward hope and growth and lasting change. There is power to do just that in your tongue!

Choose one or two unkind phrases or words you have spoken to loved ones in your home. Now, in the workbook pages, consider a better response.

Chapter 26 —
As They Grow
in Independence

Amber

As I sat working on my laptop in the living room, I heard a thunderous sound from the kitchen. I leaped from my armchair and headed toward the noise only to find my seven-year-old standing next to the microwave with the door open, two packets of ketchup from a fast food restaurant steaming in his hands. Needless to say, we had a mini science lesson on the effects of metal in microwaves. Thankfully, the microwave was no worse for the wear.

It was the beginning of summer and I realized that my boys were getting old enough to handle more of their own food prep. Instead of constantly asking me for snacks, I created a shelf in the fridge and one in the pantry and stocked them with healthy foods and items they could prepare for themselves without permission. For too long, I got into the habit of doing every little thing for them instead of teaching them to help themselves. Until the microwave incident, it had been working like a charm.

The road to independence is one of the most challenging avenues for parents to navigate. How much freedom should

I give my son with technology? When is my daughter ready to make her own clothing choices? Will my child misbehave and embarrass me if he's out of my sight? What might happen to my kids if something jeopardizes their safety and I'm not there to help them? What if they put foil packets of ketchup in the microwave? *Ahem.* These are the tough questions every parent must answer, eventually.

It's natural for kids to seek out opportunities for independence. **Parents can either clip their child's wings or groom them for flight.** It's no wonder that this is a struggle. After we bring our babies home from the hospital, they rely on us for everything. Their very lives depend on us! In motorsports, a safety car or pace car is a car that limits the speed of competing cars on a racetrack in the case of a caution period such as an obstruction on the track or bad weather. At the end of the caution period, the safety car leaves the track and the competitors resume normal racing. As our children mature, conflict happens when we don't pace with them in our parenting. There is a time and place to keep close beside them, protecting them. But there is also a time and place to step aside as they enter the highway of life.

Parents can either clip their child's wings or groom them for flight.

The natural push for independence can catch us off guard. A struggle of wills will never have a winner. The first moment our children buck the system may very well be the time to upgrade the system. Maybe it's even time to carefully maneuver your pace car off the track. It will feel a bit risky to expand your carefully constructed borders, but it's important to get comfortable with the discomfort. Find solace in knowing God will never leave you hanging when you ask Him for wisdom and discernment to know how far to extend those boundary lines or leave them on the track to finish their own race. Proverbs 2:6 assures us He is our best source for wisdom: "For the Lord gives wisdom; from his mouth come knowledge and understanding."

Last year, I was mindlessly toasting bread and buttering it for my nine-year-old when I realized he didn't even know how to use the toaster himself. "Mom, can you butter this for me?" he asked. I looked at the crispy sourdough he held on the plate I just handed him. It was a wakeup call that I was not nurturing his independence to match his capabilities and maturity. *My bad.* There was no way I was going to let my toddler near the kitchen knives, but somewhere in those years, my firstborn grew up right under my nose. I forgot to let him into the kitchen just because I was still so used to shielding his younger siblings from harm's way. As a result, I ended up with a fully capable young man who had never been taught to push a button on a kitchen appliance. You can bet we have since made up for lost time. His future wife won't be calling me up one day to ask me why I didn't teach her husband to find his way around the kitchen.

One of the reasons we struggle to give our children the independence they both desire and need, is because of fear and worry. The Psalmist gives us a practical fix for this. In Psalm 56:3 he writes, "When I am afraid, I put my trust in you." Parents, God is worthy of our total trust. He is not an abstract being, unfamiliar with our struggle. John 3:16 says, "For God so loved the world, that he gave his only Son, that whoever believes in him should not perish but have eternal life." Imagine. The Father sent His Son, Jesus, to dangerous territory, knowing full well it would mean suffering and death. Because He loved us so dearly, God sent Him willingly, and Jesus came willingly. The Lord understands the hardship of letting go. Of course, we would never put our children in harm's way intentionally, but we can trust God to sympathize with us and help us in our quest to give our kids leeway to expand their horizons.

Another reason that parents hinder a child's self-sufficiency is because of their need to control. I admit I like to be in charge of things. It'd be easy for me to become a helicopter parent, micromanaging my children's every move, but I'd be doing them a disservice even if my heart is in the right place. While my kids are young, the stakes are low. Their youth is the prime training ground to learn from their mistakes. But I have also found that my children know instinctively what their boundaries are. My boys will climb a tree or wade out into the waves of the ocean beyond what makes me comfortable, but I have learned that they are usually capable of more than I imagine. So I bite my tongue and loosen my tether.

PARENTING SCRIPTS:

Learning to give our kids independence boils down to trust—trust in the Lord and trust in our kids. God need not prove He is trustworthy. We know it's intrinsic to His character. But if you struggle with trusting your child, give him/her something to live up to:

"Jonathan, if you honor your curfew for the next two weeks, Mom and I agree that means you are responsible enough to stay out later and we will extend your curfew by half an hour from then on."

"Maisy, whenever Dad and I ask to search your phone, you never protest or get upset. We really appreciate that you honor us like that. We think it's time that you get to have it with you twenty-four/seven, not just while you are at school so we can reach you in an emergency. Remember that newfound freedom brings with it that much more trust. We know you will use it wisely."

"Quade, let's make a deal. If you research the best places to eat on our family vacation that will take into consideration our dietary needs, we will let you pick the next road trip destination we go on."

"Charlotte, thanks for always being the first to clear your dishes and put them in the sink. I think you are ready to pick out that new puppy you have been asking for because I see how responsible you are becoming."

"Oliver, if you start buttering you own toast, I'll teach you how to make your favorite chocolate cake."

A lot of the time, I think it's just easier to do things myself, but that's a shortsighted mentality. When I find I'm either running around doing too much for my kids, or if they come to me for simple things, I train myself to say this script:

"You do it. I'll watch."

Instead of automatically swooping in like a mother hen, my kids have learned that I am their coach, helping them reach their own potential. If my kids are too big physically for a piggyback then I shouldn't be carrying their responsibilities for age-appropriate tasks on my back either. They will do the "thing" and I'll be nearby to guide them if need be.

Inwardly, there's another important script I whisper to my heart:

"I don't get to take too much credit or too much blame for my child's choices."

I want to shout this loud and clear today. Hear me out, parents. God instructs us to point our kids to Him every day, when we sit in our homes and when we butter our toast, when we walk together and talk together. (Deuteronomy 6:7).

I take this passage in Deuteronomy very seriously, but at the end of the day, we are never responsible for what our children do with their lives. We are responsible for teaching them the way and the truth. Our stewardship of these precious lives will be taken into account with the Lord, but what our sons and daughters do with that knowledge and guidance is between them and the Lord. If they abuse the privileges we give them, it's our responsibility to lovingly correct them, but the ownership for wrongdoing lies only with them.

So often, moms come to me with shame in their eyes, beating themselves up over their black sheep who makes one disastrous move after another. Just today a grieving mom asked me to pray for her wayward teen. It's painful enough to watch them travel the broken road. There is no need to add our own guilty feelings to the mix. And then there are the parents who ooze with a judgmental spirit because their kids rarely do wrong. Their haughty eyes make other parents feel two feet tall. The fact of the matter is that in this too there must be balance. Don't allow your child's sin to cripple you or their righteousness to commend you. One is the thorn of yielding to Satan's temptations, the other is the fruit of Christ alone. Each is the child's own to bear. The result of grasping this truth is freedom. Freedom from comparison and condemnation. In her book, *Mom Set Free*, Jeannie Cunnion says:

You have been set free from being perfect for your children. Jesus has already accomplished a perfection that you can rest in. To parent in the "unforced rhythms of His grace," (Matt 11:28-30 MSG) we need to accept the Good News that our children's hearts are not wholly dependent on our performance as a parent. We need to accept that what we get right and what we get wrong is not what will ultimately determine who our children will become" (20,21)!

Most of us probably appreciate the grace of God for our salvation, but let's apply the boundless grace of God to our parenting too. Rid your heart of fear and the need to control the outcome of another individual, even if he is your precious child. As Christ-followers, our kids are not a reflection of us. They, like all believers, should be a reflection of their Savior.

SCRIPT-URE:

"For the Lord gives wisdom; from his mouth come knowledge and understanding"

(Proverbs 2:6)

PRAYER SCRIPT:

Father, I just want to be a good mom/dad. My desire is to raise my child to know you and to live a righteous life that honors You. It's hard to let them grow up sometimes, but I know it is best for them and for me. Help me to have wisdom to know how and when to give them the independence they need. No matter where they go or what they do, I know Your loving eyes are on them, protecting them. Thank You, Lord, for always being near. Remove my fears and my pride. Remind me that You are sovereign over their lives. Help me to nurture them with just the right amount of guidance and freedom. In Jesus' name, amen!

MAKE THE SCRIPT YOUR OWN:

What is the hardest part of seeing your child grow up? Do you tend to be too lenient or too controlling? Do you need to give them more independence? What might that look like right now? Next year? In the workbook pages, write out your own script for when your child needs more independence that fits your own family dynamics.

Chapter 27 — When Satan's Been Prowling Around Your Family

Wendy

My son Caleb wasn't more than ten years old the night he read the story of Samuel for the first time. Samuel himself was a boy in this particular story, living in the temple with Eli the old priest. Samuel's mother Hannah had been heartsick with barrenness and prayed for Samuel, fervently and with great faith. When the Lord heard her cry for a child, He opened her womb and allowed her to conceive. Nine months later, Hannah dedicated the boy to the Lord, and when he was weaned, his mother took him to the temple to be raised by Eli.

Caleb read the story of when the Lord called to young Samuel during the night as he slept. The boy got out of bed, answering, "What is it? I'm listening." Over and over again the Lord called. And over and over again the boy responded, stumbling from his cot until he found Eli, sure that Eli had called to him. Eventually, Eli figured out it was the Lord who was calling Samuel.

I pray I always remember my own boy's face all lit up and his clear voice telling me that the same thing happened to him. "God called my name before when I was in bed! I heard Him, and even thought it was dad before, but I know that it was God."

Fast-forward a handful of years later to the night this same child came to my bedside, having heard a different voice calling his name. Fear gripped him as he made his way down the dark hall to our room. "I heard a voice calling me," my teen cried, "but it wasn't God's voice. It was evil. Please pray for me."

His father and I both were up in an instant and together we walked him back to his room. And as we walked I spoke truth to our son's heart.

PARENTING SCRIPT:

I spoke the script my mother spoke over me the night I went to her bedroom over thirty years ago, crying, "There's a baby elephant sitting on my chest in my bed tonight, and he won't leave and I'm frightened."

She took me in her arms and spoke one word, one name: "Jesus."

I repeated, "Jesus."

Thirty years later I taught my child to speak the same name when the enemy comes calling. "Repeat after me, son: Jesus."

"Jesus."

"Jesus, you are a strong tower, everyone who runs into You is safe. You protect us from our enemies."

"You're a strong tower, Jesus, and I'm running into you," my child breathed the words as we all crawled into his bed together.

"Jesus," I continued, "You do not sleep nor slumber."

"You never sleep, Jesus."

"Jesus, You will fight for me, I need only to be still, Jesus."

Caleb rested in my arms and moaned before repeating, "I need only to be still, Jesus, You will fight for me."

"And Jesus ..." my words trailed off as I was overcome by emotion, so my husband finished the next one for us, "When I am afraid I will trust in You, in God whose Word I praise, in God I trust."

Caleb confessed, "I trust You, Jesus. When I'm afraid I trust You, Jesus."

And with the name of Jesus on our lips, our script in times of demonic warfare, my child fell asleep in my arms. My child, the one who intimately knows the voice of his Shepherd, knew when the voice in his ear was the deceiver. And he knew where to come for help, and I taught him the script that my own mother taught me.

"Jesus."

In the past few years I've felt the Lord call me, very clearly, to go to battle *for* my children, not against them. He's made it clear to my heart that this war is to be waged not against the people in our homes but the enemy who prowls about us, looking to steal and destroy. Since that's the case, I need to do battle with spiritual weapons rather than earthly ones! And so do you.

Many books have been written on the importance of armoring up spiritually and biblically as Christians, but I've yet to find one that applies the armor to each hard parenting day. Let's do that now with the help of Ephesians 6:10-18.

"Finally, be strong in the Lord and in the strength of his might. Put on the whole armor of God, that you may be able to stand against the schemes of the devil. For we do not wrestle against flesh and blood, but against the rulers, against the authorities, against the cosmic powers over this present darkness, against the spiritual forces of evil in the heavenly places. Therefore take up the whole armor of God, that you may be able to withstand in the evil day, and having done all, to stand firm. Stand therefore, having fastened on the belt of truth, and having put on the breastplate of righteousness, and, as shoes for your feet, having put on the readiness given by the gospel of peace. In all circumstances take up the shield of faith, with which you can extinguish all the flaming darts of the evil one; and take the helmet of salvation, and the sword of the Spirit, which is the word of God, praying at all times in the Spirit, with all prayer and supplication."

Here's a quick breakdown for the moms and dads who want to fight for their children not with them:

Verse 10 - Since this is a spiritual battle, our earthly might isn't enough. We need the Lord's strength to win this war.

Verse 11-12 - Our enemy is Satan—not our kids, not our spouse, not the school district, or a diagnosis, or our in-laws. The devil is the problem. Evil demons in this present darkness are the problem.

Verse 13 - Therefore we need to be ready to fight him, not them.

Verse 14 - Wear truth as a belt, because truth keeps the rest of the armor girded up and in place! And put your breastplate of righteousness over your heart to protect that vulnerable emotional sphere.

Verse 15 - Lace up your gospel shoes, ready to walk your salvation out step by step right in their midst. The gospel is Jesus. Extend His forgiveness and grace and salvation and new mercies and the fruit of His Spirit day after day. Walk that out with your kids regardless of how they walk. Keep those gospel shoes on!

Verse 16 - Hold up your faith like a shield of defense. Even the smallest mustard seed-sized faith can withstand the enemy's attacks, so hold it up high like a banner of belief. Don't let it falter. Don't let your faith fall.

Verse 17 - Pick up the Word of God, which is your strongest weapon, and wield it daily! Read God's Word, believe God's Word, speak it, and pray it, and attack our enemy with it when he tempts you with lies. And don't forget to cover your mind with the helmet of salvation before blazing into battle. Imagine your helmet like a bowl before you in your hands, filled with the cleansing blood of Christ. Put it on and let the blood cover your thinking and your perceiving, even your ears and eyes and your mouth, your hearing and seeing and speaking.

Verse 18 - And pray. Armor up and pray. Battle when you rise and when you lie down and when you do the dishes and when you drive them to school and when you take them to the ball field and when you wake up in cold-sweats in the middle of the night, pray the name of Jesus.

We have been given authority by Jesus Christ to pray for our children in His name.

Ask the Lord if there are any evil, oppressive spirits that are making mischief in your children's lives. Ask Him how to pray His Word as you apply it and believe it. Ask Him to reveal any and all generational sin that needs to be rebuked in His name so new blessings can flow into your children's hearts and into your home. Ask the Lord for spiritual eyes to see and a mind to perceive how to pray for them. Ask for clarity and discernment, wisdom and an abundance of love to cover all sins.

And pray.

God's Spirit is faithful to answer the prayers of moms and dads. Every day His Spirit speaks to the spirits of interceding parents as they fast and pray on behalf of their family members.

So pray and fast.

> *"And when they came to the multitude, a man came up to Him, falling on his knees before Him, and saying, "Lord, have mercy on my son, for he is a lunatic, and is very ill; for he often falls into the fire, and often into the water. And I brought him to Your disciples, and they could not cure him." And Jesus answered and said, "O unbelieving and perverted generation, how long shall I be with you? How long shall I put up with you? Bring him here to Me." And Jesus rebuked him, and the demon came out of him, and the boy was cured at once.*
>
> *Then the disciples came to Jesus privately and said, "Why could we not cast it out?" And He said to them, "Because of the littleness of your faith; for truly I say to you, if you have faith as a mustard seed, you shall say to this mountain, 'Move from here to there,' and it shall move; and nothing shall be impossible to you. [But this kind does not go out except by prayer and fasting]" (Matthew 17:14-21, NASB).*

Did you catch that? The man who came to Jesus in this story was a parent! Let that sink in. Parents can come to Jesus and do battle by faith *today*.

Moms and dads, I said it before and will say it again, I know that the tendency on weary parenting days is for us to fight with our children, but God has told us that our battle is not with them! **We have a real enemy.** He'll attack our relationships, our finances, our health, and even our kids if he thinks it will undo our spiritual legacy. We have an enemy who is hell-bent on destroying our children, along with our testimonies, and our *We have a real* family legacies of faith. Therefore, we *enemy.* armor up and stand against the devil's evil schemes with the full authority that Christ has given us through faith and say, "Satan, get behind me! Get behind us all." Then pray.

PRAYER SCRIPT:

"Jesus, You have told me that when I resist the devil, he has to flee! And so I bind him in Your name and send him to Your feet. I rebuke him on behalf of my family and renounce any hold he has over my children. I take back any foothold he has ever taken and cut him off from ever entering our home again. He may not touch my children, my spouse, our home, our car, our thinking, or our speaking. We have been bought with the blood of Christ and plead His blood over our family—His blood is an impenetrable shield, protecting us both now and forevermore! In Jesus' name, power, and authority I pray, amen!"

And then, parents, I encourage you to bless your children. Think of their little beings as garden plots. You've just removed weeds and now you get to plant righteous seeds in the fertile soil of your family life.

"Lord I bless my children with faith, power, and a sound mind in Jesus Christ. I bless my marriage with kindness and love. I

bless our home with a spirit of unity, generosity, and service. I bless each one of us with a sense of Your Holy Spirit's abiding nearness. I bless the generations to come with love, joy, and peace through faith, until our Savior returns! In the blessed name of Jesus, who has set us free! Amen."

Take yourself humbly now to the throne of God for Jesus has allowed us that privilege. Come to Him, fast from anything that distracts your prayer life, and pray in the power and authority that Christ has given you through faith. Pray for your children with the most powerful prayer script of all: Jesus.

SCRIPT-URE:

"For our struggle is not against flesh and blood, but against the rulers, against the authorities, against the powers of this dark world and against the spiritual forces of evil in the heavenly realms"

(Ephesians 6:12)

MAKE THE SCRIPT YOUR OWN:

Have you felt the devil prowling around your family? Do you believe God has given you the authority to rebuke him on behalf of your children, in the name of Jesus? He has through faith. In the workbook pages, I encourage you to pray—whether you feel led to write your own prayer script or simply copy the ones included in this chapter. Go on now, make this script your own. Amen?

Chapter 28 —
When They Take the
Easy Way Out

Amber

I could have sworn I told my kids to put their dirty socks out by the laundry machine in the garage and yet there they were, scattered haphazardly around the house. One was even hanging from a lamp. "Boys!" I called out. The next few minutes involved slow moving kids mumbling their way through a load of laundry. It's not like this was the first time we have had the sock conversation. And yet my kids need coaching in this area often. It's not because they don't remember. It's because becoming a person who is faithful in the little things means practicing the discipline of it over and over and over again in preparation to be faithful in the big things.

Of course, plenty of kids become adults who still prefer easy street. What can we do to deter them from that route? When we equip our kids to develop a strong work ethic in the everyday tasks of life, we prepare them to establish a strong spiritual ethic too. Never has this been more important than in our world today. The longer I'm alive, the more persecution I witness and the more I have to endure myself. I hear from parents who fear that once their children enter the real world, they will walk away from God. One of my most fervent prayers is that my kids will not take the easy way out when it comes to small things so that they will instinctively be prepared to stand strong in the spiritual realms as they mature. When I teach them to put their socks in the laundry basket, it's not just because I want them to be organized. It's because I want them to be characterized by integrity and a willingness to go the extra mile. Engaging in conflict instead of coaching them when they settle for mediocre keeps kids in training wheels instead of behind the wheel of responsibility.

All too often my kids make the excuse that they don't want to do something because it's too hard. You may have heard the saying, "We can do hard things!" I love that thought, but as Christ-followers, I want my kids to take that idea one step further. We can do the hard things, certainly, but the hard thing is often the right thing. I don't want them to avoid doing what is right just because it's a challenge. Spiritual tenacity is only one decision away, and in my efforts to raise kids with character, they often hear me say this:

PARENTING SCRIPT:

"The hard thing is often the right thing."

Jesus never said that following Him would be a picnic. On the contrary, in I Peter 2:21, it says, "For to this you have been called, because Christ also suffered for you, leaving you an example, so that you might follow in his steps." The math is simple, but the application is not. Jesus plus His suffering equals our example. The lot of the Christian is that he will be tested and tried. The end result is an eternal reward and joy despite our earthly circumstances. While the reward is high, it's not one that we or our kids would naturally choose to pay the price for. This is why we must be committed as parents to help our kids do the hard things.

People who don't take the easy way out are people who embrace two things: courage and selflessness. Let's examine courage for a moment. One of my favorite stories in the Bible highlights the bravery of three young men who displayed the kind of valor that is the stuff of heroes. In 600 BC, Shadrach, Meshach, and Abednego were put to the test. Mighty and powerful King Nebuchadnezzar built an idol made of gold that towered over the land. Everyone under his reign, many thousands and thousands of subjects, were commanded to bow down to this idol at the first note of music that played. The penalty for not bowing down was certain death upon being thrown into a fiery furnace. These three teens would not bow and even though Nebuchadnezzar gave them a second chance to obey, they stood their ground and stood tall:

"Shadrach, Meshach and Abednego replied to him, 'KingNebuchadnezzar, we do not need to defend ourselves before you in this matter. If we are thrown into the blazing furnace, the God we serve is able to deliver us from it, and he will deliver us from Your Majesty's hand. But even if he does not, we want you to know, Your Majesty, that we will not serve your gods or worship the image of gold you have set up'" (Daniel 3:16-18, NIV).

I guarantee you courage like that doesn't develop overnight. These young men had a history of doing the right thing over and over and over again. We know because earlier in Daniel chapter 1, Shadrach, Meshach, and Abednego, along with their friend Daniel did not take the easy way out, giving in to pleasure for a season. They were chosen to be trained for the king's service and were told to partake of the rich and delectable foods of Babylon. Instead, they chose the hard path. They made this request:

> *"Please test your servants for ten days: Give us nothing but vegetables to eat and water to drink. Then compare our appearance with that of the young men who eat the royal food, and treat your servants in accordance with what you see.' So he agreed to this and tested them for ten days. At the end of the ten days they looked healthier and better nourished than any of the young men who ate the royal food. So the guard took away their choice food and the wine they were to drink and gave them vegetables instead"* (Daniel 1:12-17).

Becoming a vegetarian was child's play compared to facing cremation, but it was these kind of difficult choices that prepared them for the test of their lives. God honored their faithfulness at every turn. Each time we stand up for what we believe in, our faith increases in order to prepare us for the next occasion. This is what I want my children to practice under my watchful eye.

The second quality of someone who does not take the easy way out is selflessness. When I picture the Lord Jesus, I see a man who had no care for His own comfort. He was and is servant of all: "For even the Son of Man came not to be served but to serve, and to give his life as a ransom for many" (Matthew 10:45). Can you imagine what transformation would take place if everyone in our homes applied this measure of selflessness? We would be eager to do the hard things because **the intensity of the task is not how we measure our willingness**. Performance would not be the product of punishment or persuasion. It would be the fruit of the Spirit. It would be the purpose behind our actions and the pleasure of our hearts. However, for service

the intensity of the task is not how we measure our willingness.

to become second nature, it must be ingrained in us, one self-denial and one sock in the washer at a time.

My son stands before me, protesting a simple task that he perceives is too hard. My response is said firmly with love, as I remind him, "The hard thing is often the right thing, Son." I know I'm not just teaching him life skills. I'm fueling his heart to burn for the greater things so he may not be tempted to bow down to the pressures of the world or the whims of an earthly king because he is already committed to the King of Kings.

SCRIPT-URE:

"For to this you have been called, because Christ also suffered for you, leaving you an example, so that you might follow in his steps"

(I Peter 2:21)

PRAYER SCRIPT:

Lord Jesus, You are the King of kings and the Lord of lords and yet You became a humble man to show us how to be like You. I want my kids to be strong for You and not be tempted to take the easy path. Lord, fill them with Your might so they will stand strong in a world that keeps trying to make them bow low. Use me to teach them and coach them to do the hard things because they are the right things. May You be glorified and may we be sanctified. In Jesus' name, amen!

MAKE THE SCRIPT YOUR OWN:

Identify two areas where your child tends to take the easy road. What would their excuses be? Are you tempted to give up and take the easy road in your parenting as you attempt to train your kids? In the workbook pages, write out your own script for when your child takes the easy way out that fits your own family dynamics.

Chapter 29 —
When You're Not Parenting
on the Same Page
(AKA - Marriage Scripts)

Wendy

"He works such long hours …"

"I'm the one who's always with the kids …"

"She reacts emotionally, and makes everything into such a big deal …"

"It's hard for me to let him deal with problems, because he doesn't do it theway I want him to …"

"She freaks out over nothing …"

"He doesn't have time to read good parenting books…

"Her parents were terribly abusive, and I can hear her mother's voice when she corrects our kids …

"He's too harsh …

"She's too lenient …

"It's just easier for me to discipline the kids ..."

Amber and I receive plenty of emails from moms and dads, husbands and wives, even divorced couples who long to parent unified. The common problem is that one parent wants to do one thing in moments of correction when the other parent does the exact opposite. One parent will fly off the handle, while the other sulks and sighs. One spouse will use Scripture to discipline a child, and the other spouse will berate or yell. One parent believes in spanking, while the other adult in the house was abused under the banner of such discipline. One parent tries to figure out natural consequences and punishments that fit each crime, while the other parent threatens incessantly to remove a child's electronics, no matter what the offense.

Here in the pages of this book, we talk (a lot) about coming up with gentle responses together; however, the simple truth is that before you can parent unified, you have to be unified. And that too takes planning. If the thought of making a plan with your children's other parent feels impossible (because of all the fighting or their passive aggressive communication style), I'm sorry for the stress it causes you both and the kids too. But let's press on, believing that with God even this is possible (Matthew 19:26).

Moms often include in their messages to us that they'd like their spouse to read one of our books. As a matter of fact, it was because of these letters that we decided to publish audio versions of both *Triggers* and *Parenting Scripts*. Their husbands, we heard time and again, would be more likely to listen to a few chapters on their way to work than read them when they got home.

Either way, listening or reading, what women are saying is that they want desperately to parent on the same page with their husbands. Having a book that speaks to both of you, that gives you tools to use and prayers to pray, that provides you with pages upon which to stand as common ground, is paramount. And so, at the end of each of these chapters, when you get to the part that says MAKE THE SCRIPT YOUR OWN, followed by a blank page to fill, what we want for you to do is to talk it through together if at all possible.

In a moment void of conflict (not in the middle of the stress), meet-up and come up with some ideas that fit you both. If you're in a strained relationship with your ex, perhaps a cordial (well prayed over) email that starts, "I could use your help. I'm trying to make some plans about how I want to parent our son when he ..." or "Have you noticed that our daughter is ... I'd like to talk it through with you so we can help her through this difficult stage together as a team."

Many of you women married men who plan their calendar year around sports. Some dads require their family to go to the early service at church in the fall so they can hustle home directly after the doxology to the couch for kick-off. Then there's March Madness and spring fever ...

If anyone understands the imagery of working together as a team, it's these guys. Nobody wins the game when there's dissension on the field, and nobody wins in the home when we're trying to score in two different nets. Proverbs 29:18 in the King James Version describes it this way, "Where there is no vision, the people perish." We need a shared vision about how to win as a family! Of course the best time to come up with a unified game plan isn't on the sidelines in between innings, but carefully and prayerfully before the next game. That's the heart of this book. And this chapter, we pray, will help to unify your team.

Before we start, I'd like to write plainly to the men: I'm about to spend a few paragraphs affirming the way God made you and encouraging the mother of your children to trust you. But I need to preface that with this strong word: If you know deep in your spirit that you struggle with anger and abusive behavior, you need to get help. Reach out to your pastor, to a therapist, to the godly men in your life. Before I exhort your masculine design and the strength God wove into your fibers, we must recognize that men are called to servant-leadership, loving and leading as Christ loves and leads the church (Ephesians 5:25).

A man's God-given strength was given for good and fruitful purposes—to love and lead his family, not to abuse it. Often men balk at conversations of gentleness, thinking gentleness and kindness and love and patience are adjectives reserved for moms, not dads, but that's not true. The fruit of God's Spirit is available to all who abide in Him.

In his book, *The Fruitful Life*, Jerry Bridges affirms men in their calling to be gentle with these words:

> *"Men often want to see gentleness in their mothers and wives, but not in themselves. The macho image of the non-Christian male world has a tendency to rub off, even on us. But the apostle Paul uses the example of a mother's gentleness to describe his own character. He was able to say to the Thessalonian believers, 'We were gentle among you, like a mother caring for her little children'" (1 Thessalonians 2:7).*

This is the foundation of how we want to treat one another (both in marriage and in parenting). That said, men and women are different. A man's muscular design is different than a woman's. Their hormones are different. Their roles in society and in the church are different. And yet the call to bear this spiritual fruit remains the same.

That's hard, I imagine. Because of their physical and chemical design, it's common for men to get angry quickly! So the question for husbands and dads is this: **How do you temper your temper?** The best advice I can give you doesn't come from me, but from my own masculine husband who shows me the answer every morning when I wake up and he's already got his Bible open on the couch in the living room. Husbands, dads, men, you need to spend time with Jesus so you live like Jesus, love like Jesus, and lead like Jesus each day.

Jesus wasn't a white-robed wimp. While He is our Prince of Peace. He's also the warrior God who will one day return on the back of a stallion, wielding a sword. He's the One who got angry, yet didn't sin. Fully God, yet fully man. And He's the Man you need to speak with, man-to-man, every day.

And ladies, we need our husbands and the fathers of our children to be men. In a culture laden with gender neutrality, we need our men to lead as men. God gave them an extra measure of muscle, infused them with testosterone, and put in their chests a warrior's heart, and then charged them to love and lead with their God-purposed strength. What an incredible call upon a man's life: to lead his family as Christ leads the church—gently, protectively, sacrificially, demonstratively, with strength and humility. It's complicated! They need our prayers and support more than our judgment and correction.

I spent some time with a family friend recently, an older man who raised half a dozen sons of his own. Because I have three masculine boys, all cut from their father's strong cloth, I pulled my chair up close to his. After I went on for a while about the reality in our "testosterhome" (as Amber puts it), he started to laugh, affirming that while they need correction, everything I shared was normal. Then he asked me, point blank, "Do you let your husband handle them when they're acting up?"

Of course, I was about to say, then stopped. "He's harsher in his tone than I am." I began. "And he doesn't always use words that build them up."

"When?" he asked.

"When they're ignoring him or complaining about yard work mostly." I answered.

He let the silence do a work between us for a while before saying, "I can tell you're purposeful as their mom, to speak life over your kids, and that's good. And dads need to do the same. But sometimes, and oftentimes for some kids, they need their dad to be strong and clear and not so very affirming when they've done wrong. You and your husband, together, paint a picture of God the Father who is both gentle and merciful but also strong and quick and just. I'd like to encourage you to take a step back and let your husband do his job. Let him handle it. As long as he's not abusing you and the children, you all need him to be the dad God made him to be."

Let him handle it, the words rolled over in my mind as I drove home that afternoon. That night I asked some friends what they thought, and one gal responded, "Our rule is, 'Let whoever's handling it, handle it.'" I smiled, because it was a pithy little script I knew I could remember.

"*Let whoever's handling it, handle it.*"

"Let whoever's handling it, handle it."

I thought of the times I've quickened my pace on my way to the kitchen when I've overheard my husband correcting the boys, and how I attempt to take over. And those times we're in the car and the children keep interrupting our front seat conversation. When their dad corrects with a strong statement, rather than a motherly tone, I need to remember "Let whoever's handling it, handle it."

Ladies, we don't want to emasculate our men. They're not supposed to speak to our children like we speak to our children. While we both need to bear the fruit of God's Spirit in our lives, these men shouldn't sound like us. They need to speak to our children as men, not as women. Whether your family is made up of boys or girls, or a mix of the two, they need a mother's voice and a father's.

"Yes, Wendy, but what if his masculine soil is too rocky and he doesn't have any gentle fruit growing in his life? What if he can't handle the kids without hurting them? Do I still let him handle it?" I can hear many of you asking me these hard questions, even as I write. So here's my answer:

If you believe that his masculine approach is simply too harsh for you and the kids at times, then you may need to script an invitation. This is not a fight, but an invitation to talk it through. And likewise, men, if you feel strongly about her words and tone and feel the need to confront, make a plan to do so gently. Just as we are learning to do with our children, we need to apply the lesson with one another. Make a plan, so that you can speak the truth to one another, lovingly (Ephesians 4:15).

Husbands, this can be difficult for you because generally speaking men tend to address the facts without the feelings. "You do this every day, and it's wrong and hurtful and probably comes from the way your own mother ..." And on it rolls, a steady, hurtful stream of honesty. And some of you women might have the tendency to launch a quick counter-attack, using your entire arsenal of words all at once. This type of war never leads to a family victory.

That said, many wives struggle with the opposite issue: not saying anything at all in their attempt to submit. (By the way, this is my natural tendency). However, the Lord has given us clear direction as to how all believers can and should address sin-struggles with love—in the church and even in marriage. When there's sin to confront in the life of a fellow believer, the Word clearly instructs us to do so with humility and love. And if that "fellow believer" is our spouse? The same instruction applies: approach them humbly and lovingly. "Brothers, if anyone is caught in any transgression, you who are spiritual should restore him in a spirit of gentleness. Keep watch on yourself, lest you too be tempted. Bear one another's burdens, and so fulfill the law of Christ" (Galatians 6:1-2).

Unfortunately, "humbly" and "lovingly" doesn't always come naturally, so you've got to make that plan.

Whether you are the mom or the dad, here are two things you can do when you're not parenting on the same page.

1. **Pray** - The first thing to do is pray. This is another bit of advice straight from my own husband's lips: "Pray for me, Wendy. Pray for me when I sin, and then let the Holy Spirit affirm it in my heart." I can't tell you how many miracle stories have played out in our home when I've prayed in the morning, and he's come home convicted and repentant that night. What a beautiful picture of 1 Peter 3:1-2.

   "In the same way, you wives, be submissive to your own husbands so that even *if any of them are disobedient to the word*, they may be won without a word by the behavior of their wives, as they observe your chaste and respectful behavior" (1 Peter 3:1-2, NASB, italics added for emphasis).

   Ladies, cover your children's dad in prayer. When he does wrong, reacting in sin and selfishness, fight for him on your knees, prayerfully, tirelessly. And if he continues to be "disobedient to the word" of God, you still don't need to jump in and start swinging your words at him. Remain respectful and carefully plan your next step.

2. **Correct in love** - If the sin continues, and the Lord puts it on your heart to confront him, then do so in love, in a moment void of conflict. Look to God's Word and make a plan, then write out the script of what you want to say. Here are some marriage scripts to inspire you and some Scriptures to equip you.

MARRIAGE SCRIPTS:

Plan your invitation: "I've noticed that when the kids do (insert wrong behavior here) you and I both struggle to know what to do. I try this and you try that, and nothing seems to be working. Can we steal away some afternoon this week and grab a coffee and make a plan together? I really want to be unified on this."

When confronting differences, but not necessarily sin, make sure to use "I" statements rather than "you" accusations. And steer clear from the phrase "you always …" The goal is to be reconciled not ridiculed. Try, "Honey, when the kids are ignoring us and you get angry, I feel anxious. And I don't see that the yelling actually gets to our kids' hearts. They might come to the table or finish cleaning their rooms, but it doesn't help them to obey next time or to bring us together as a family. I don't have a better plan yet, but I'd like to make one. Would you help me to make a plan, so we can try to get to their hearts when they're doing wrong and not just get them to obey in that moment?"

When confronting sin: "I want you to know I have been praying for you a lot lately. I've been praying that God would bless you and speak to you and give you all you need at work and at home. As I've prayed, I've felt led to speak to you about (insert sin here). God's Word tells me that when a fellow believer has sin in their life, we are to gently confront them.

I know this is hard for you to hear. Believe me, it's hard for me to say it, but I believe that your (name sin) is a sin problem. I'm not angry at you. I've been forgiven of my own sins countless times, by both God and you, so I'm not judging you, but I am confronting you in love. We don't need to talk this through right now, but I want you to know I am praying for you and needed to tell you.

Husbands and wives, moms and dads, there is victory for you as you parent. But it requires teamwork.

SCRIPT-URE:

"Where there is no vision, the people perish"
(Proverbs 29:18, KJV)

PRAYER SCRIPT:

Dear Lord, thank You for being so intentional when You made men and women differently. Help us to understand what that means in our parenting. I want to respect those differences. Please, Holy Spirit, give me the self-control needed to stand back and trust You when my husband/wife is parenting. Bless our family by supernaturally giving us a shared vision for how You want us to parent together. And if and when there is sin in our parenting, I ask You to convict us quickly and kindly. We'll need clarity and courage to confront one another during those times, but we trust that with You it's possible. Thank You. I ask this all in Your precious name, amen.

MAKE THE SCRIPT YOUR OWN:

Are you parenting on the same page with your children's other parent? Or is there so much discord you're never able to come up with a solution to any problem? It's time to write out an invitation then reach out and ask them to make a plan with you. Let them know that you value their strengths and need their help. Communicate your plan to not rush in and run interference on their plays from now on. In the workbook pages, make a game plan together, so that you are parenting on the same page.

Chapter 30 —
When They Need to
Know You Love Them

Amber

"But Mom," he whimpered. "Please. I take it back." The most atrocious words had been streaming from his mouth all morning. It was unlike him, but for the last week his feelings of entitlement had been on full display. Grace upon grace had been offered him, and as he ate the breakfast I made for him, put on the clothing I bought for him, and prepared to ride to school with his best friend that I had arranged for him, he spoke with some of the worst disrespect I had ever heard.

We had ten minutes to get in the car before I dropped him and his brother off at the carpool where my friend was going to take her son and mine to the donut shop as a special treat before school. There was no way I was going to allow my boy to believe he could continue with his sinful behavior and receive a blessing. You see, Wendy and I believe in giving our kids what they don't deserve on a regular basis. The grace that saved us often manifests in benevolence, even when our kids misbehave. Our desire to draw them with loving-kindness means we don't pound the gavel like a judge for every infraction. Their sin or immaturity needs careful attention from us. Holy Spirit discernment reveals to us which situations need natural consequences or discipline and which scenarios are teachable moments where our loving-kindness will serve to draw their hearts to repentance.

In *Triggers*, I write that obedience gives birth to blessing. My kids know things will go well for them when they obey and that when they don't, they will be the ones who rob themselves of the good God has in store for them. My son took one look at the shock on my face over his insolent mouth, and he knew he had crossed a line. I was thankful he understood there was a line to cross, but nonetheless, there he stood, just beyond the boundary.

"Son, go ahead and get your backpack," I said to his brother. "I'll drive you to meet up with Susan for donuts." I turned to the offender and said my favorite parenting script of all:

"I love you."

He needed to know in the midst of his sin, he was loved. I went on:

"And because I love you, I will not allow you to go down a wrong path." I say it firmly. Passionately. *Imploringly.*

"You know I want to grace you every chance I get but God gave you to me to watch over and love. And to correct you! You will not be going to school with your friend or getting donuts this morning." I informed him. And with that, I left him crying woefully to his father as I stepped out to take his brother to our meet up spot.

Your sin never affects just you. It will often impact the people around you.

The car ride was tearful too. His brother lamented not getting to spend

224

this special time together, and I tucked that away in my heart to share when I got home: **"Your sin never affects just you. It will often impact the people around you.** The people you love. It's another thing to consider before you make a wrong choice. The blessing of obedience doesn't just slip through your fingers, it feels like a fist to the stomach for those who are sucker punched by your wrong choices."

I pulled the car into the driveway and collected his things. Silently, he followed me back out to the car so I could drive him to class. I shared the parenting scripts I had prepared, and he listened. *Really listened.* The pain of missing out on a fun morning got his attention. The sound of his breathing was labored as he tried to compose himself, and I passed back a cool wet wipe to ease the redness around his eyes.

"Remember my darling, I love you. There will be another opportunity to experience the blessing of donuts with friends," I tell him as we climb out of the car and make our way down the hallway toward his classroom. That afternoon, he came to me with his apology. He mended his relationship with me, though he knew there was nothing that he could do to decrease my love for him. The following week he earned the privilege of a donut run with his buddy, and he didn't take it for granted.

One of my heart's desires is that my children would have a crystal clear picture of their heavenly Father's love for them. It is magnificent in its grace, but sometimes grace looks like discipline. Proverbs 3:12 says, "For the LORD corrects those he loves, just as a father corrects a child in whom he delights" (NLT).

When I carefully consider how to display God's love for my children in everyday moments, the description in I Corinthians 13:4-7, *The Message*, makes it clear:

"Love never gives up.
Love cares more for others than for self.
Love doesn't want what it doesn't have.
Love doesn't strut,
Doesn't have a swelled head,
Doesn't force itself on others,
Isn't always "me first,"
Doesn't fly off the handle,
Doesn't keep score of the sins of others,
Doesn't revel when others grovel,
Takes pleasure in the flowering of truth,
Puts up with anything,
Trusts God always,
Always looks for the best,
Never looks back,
But keeps going to the end."

There are many occasions when my favorite script comes into play from day to day like this:

"Because I love you, we won't be going to the park today. I know you need rest and this would be one too many things to pack into our schedule."

"I want you to know I'm looking for ways I can be kind to you today, because I love you and love is kind."

"No, darling, we can't have another piece of cake. I love you too much to allow you to fill your body with that much sugar which could make you sick."

"Because I love you, I'm going to forgive you right now, even if you decide not to apologize. Love is forgiving and love never keeps a record of wrongs, so I'm not going to hold this against you. I just wanted you to know."

"Love is not impatient, so let me know how much time you need to finish your chore and let's make a plan together. I love you, and I want to show you that I can be patient. That's what love does."

At times the script is internal. When your child is struggling with her homework and you become exasperated, this internal script works to remind you that love bears all things so you can lovingly bear down and help her through her work. Or in those hard seasons when there is very little promise that your child is going to change for the better, remind yourself that love believes the best and trusts God for the outcome. Wendy will describe more internal scripts in the next chapter, but don't underestimate the power of speaking life into your own heart too.

With every parenting script, the foundation must be love. It was love that rescued us from our own childish desires, and it was love that matured us toward Christ-likeness. God can mold our kids into passionate Christ-followers without us, but what a blessing to be the one who gives them that understanding because love lived within the walls of their home and on the edges of our lips.

SCRIPT-URE:

"For the LORD corrects those he loves, just as a father corrects a child in whom he delights"

(Proverbs 3:12, NLT)

PRAYER SCRIPT:

Heavenly Father, thank You for Your unconditional love for me and my child. You are love. In every interaction with me, You are loving, and I want my son/daughter to feel my love, even when I have to correct and discipline them. Help me to model what love looks like so they will have an accurate understanding of who You are. Thank you for taking my feeble attempts and making them effective. Lord, I need to feel Your love for me today. Reveal it to me in a special way. In Jesus' name, amen!

MAKE THE SCRIPT YOUR OWN:

What is one recurring struggle in your home where the simple script "I love you" needs to be spoken? How did your parents communicate love to you growing up? Did that impact how you view God's love for you? What quality of love in I Corinthians 13 can you choose to focus on this week in your parenting scripts? In the workbook pages, write out your own script for the child who needs to know you love them, that fits your own family dynamics.

Chapter 31 — When You Need to Speak Truth to Your Own Heart (AKA - Internal Scripts)

Wendy

I hate this.

Those three words echoed in my mind with such regularity that one day as I folded clothes while the kids yelled at one another down the hall, they tumbled out over my lips. "I hate this …"

It shocked me to have spoken out loud what tormented me on the inside. I felt sadness and shame. My constant inner dialogue had taken root and was bearing fruit on the outside of my thought life in the form of spoken words. While none of the kids heard my confession, they had been thought and said just the same. What had been planted on the inside was bearing fruit.

The times I react in anger and frustration reveal that there is anger and frustration in me. When my innards churn with tumult, tumultuous words flow out over my lips. The moments I lack gentleness on the outside, you can be sure it's missing within, "for out of the abundance of the heart his mouth speaks" (Luke 6:45).

I write a lot about the fruit of God's Spirit displayed in our lives, and I am often convicted that the negative, unspiritual fruit that tends to grow on the branches of my personal tree is because I don't work to cultivate my thought-life with good seed and soil.

> *"You cannot be fruitful unless you remain in me" (John 15:4, NLT).*

Even our thought-life must be rooted to the vine in order to reap good fruit. Here at the close of this book, as with every other chapter, let me encourage us all to purposefully make a plan to cultivate our thought life as well.

"So, every healthy tree bears good fruit, but the diseased tree bears bad fruit. A healthy tree cannot bear bad fruit, nor can a diseased tree bear good fruit. Every tree that does not bear good fruit is cut down and thrown into the fire. Thus you will recognize them by their fruits" (Matthew 7:17-20).

If you want to grow the fruit of good words on the laurels of your life, you've got to plant them on the inside first and foremost.

Just as Amber and I have both suggested that you turn your negatives into positives when speaking to our children, we must do this with our thoughts as well. *I hate them* must be pulled out by the root. Planted in their place should be the words, *I love them. I can't do this!* needs to become, *With Christ I can!* Words like: *I suck as a mom. They'd be better off without me, I'll never get better. They never listen, why do I even try …* all need to go, and in their stead we need to speak words of life over our own hearts and minds, *I'm a wonderful mom, they are blessed to have me and I am blessed to have them. The more I spend time with God the Father, the more I become like Him. There's hope!*

When we dwell on how hard our life is, we start believing it's not fair. When we believe we're being abused by all our little people, we can lash out from the darkness of our thought life. One of the ways you can combat the darkness inside your heart and mind is replacing the "It's hard/this isn't fair" message with new words, light-drenched words purposed to dispel the darkness.

INTERNAL SCRIPT:

My favorite internal scripts are very simple. *I'm a good mom! God did a good job when He gave me my kids, and He did a good job when they gave them me! I am calm and I am kind.* And, perhaps my favorite, *I've got this, because God's got me!*

Powerful yet pithy perspective-altering words. I've whispered them over myself and said them full-voice out loud for years now, and miracle of miracles, they are taking root in my life, and bearing fruit.

You understand our encouragement to "speak the truth in love" to your children and your spouse (Ephesians 4:15), how about you learn to speak the truth in love over yourself too? What a difference it makes when you fix your thoughts on what is true and right and pure about your own heart (Philippians 4:8, NLT).

Recently, I was struggling with a negative inner-dialogue again and felt it pressing on the inside of my lips, fighting to come out. But I remembered my script, and I said it to myself and believed it too. Then something amazing happened. With the child before me, the one who was pushing for a cupcake for lunch and complaining about having to take a shower before heading to a party, my inner-dialogue bubbled out of my heart. I spoke out loud what I'd been speaking silently. Rather than those old negative feelings, "I hate this… how come you always… why can't you just…" New words flowed from me like a fount of living water. Words rooted securely in truth replaced the lies I used to believe and was tempted to speak:

"I love you son. I am a good mom. I am calm and I am kind and you can trust me to make good choices for you. I'm sorry you can't see that right now, but God did an excellent job when He made me your mom, because He knew I would help you grow up to be good and wise and kind. He also wants me to teach you to eat healthy food and wash your hair and brush your teeth. I'm doing a good job of teaching you all those things. And He wants me to hug you a lot and tell you all about how much He loves you too. I do those things too. You are so lucky to have me for a mom, and I am so blessed to have you for a son. Let's treat each other well today. You don't want to fight me, and I don't want to fight you. What do you say we hug?"

If your thoughts hurt you, your words will hurt them. So plan your words to them by scripting the words you speak to yourself. Purposefully scripted internal words will shape your spoken words.

If your thoughts hurt you, your words will hurt them. So plan your words to them by scripting the words you speak to yourself. Purposefully scripted internal words will shape your spoken words.

Here's another important reason to rescript your inner-dialogue: If you're not proactive in planning thoughts that cheer you up, your thoughts may stray to giving up.

"Not that I have already obtained this or am already perfect, but I press on to make it my own, because Christ Jesus has made me his own. Brothers, I do not consider that I have made it my own. But one thing I do: forgetting what lies behind and straining forward to what lies ahead, I press on toward the goal for the prize of the upward call of God in Christ Jesus (Philippians 3:12-14).

God's Word charges us to press on in order to win the prize for which God has called us heavenward in Christ Jesus. Press on is the call when we're tempted to call it quits. Press on, for there's a prize awaiting us when we do. The prize is both an earthly one, this side of glory, and an eternal reward on the other side of these intense days. Here on earth we are promised the joy of reaping a harvest if we do not give up (Galatians 6:9). We are promised the great joy of watching our children walk in the truth, if we don't grow weary (3 John 1:4). And eternally, we know that after we have run this race, a throne-side seat in glory awaits.

"Therefore, since we are surrounded by so great a cloud of witnesses, let us also lay aside every weight, and sin which clings so closely, and let us run with endurance the race that is set before us, looking to Jesus, the founder and perfecter of our faith, who for the joy that was set before him endured the cross, despising the shame, and is seated at the right hand of the throne of God" (Hebrews 12:1-2).

God has both present joy and an eternal joy set before us when we don't call it quits. But as is the case with every chapter in this book, it requires us to make a plan and then persist. Remain in Him, persist in Him, and you will bear fruit in your thought life and your spoken life too.

And this is where we begin to wrap up our book, with the encouragement to press on, to think what is true, and to make better plans. While this has been a journey of sorts, we know the journey does not end at the end of this book, so the call to press on continues as you think and as you plan and as you speak. Because when what we are saying isn't working, we must write a new script.

SCRIPT-URE:

"And now, dear brothers and sisters, one final thing. Fix your thoughts on what is true, and honorable, and right, and pure, and lovely, and admirable. Think about things that are excellent and worthy of praise"

(Philippians 4:8, NLT)

PRAYER SCRIPT:

Dear heavenly Father, I ask You, Lord, to speak truth into my heart tonight. Speak, Holy Spirit, to my spirit, and teach me to speak Your truth over myself. Gracious words and loving words, words that can take root in me and then bear fruit in how I live and what I say. And courage, Lord, I ask for courage to press on in right thinking and right speaking as I follow You and lead them. Thank You for being near enough to hear all of these requests, in Jesus' mighty and loving name, amen.

MAKE THE SCRIPT YOUR OWN:

Here's your final assignment: Take one lie you've believed about yourself or your children and replace it with a radical, paradigm-shifting true statement! Speak the truth in love over yourself and over your family and over all the good blessings you've been given. Think it, and speak it on the inside, and watch as it bubbles up out of you in the days ahead. For what we think we speak, so write yourself in internal script too, in the workbook pages.

Epilogue —

When my children were young and came to me fussing, I often used the simple script, "I'm sorry Honey, I don't understand you when you use that voice. Try again with a big kid voice." Over the years, as they grew bigger, the script got shorter. We cut it down to the simple phrase, "Try again."

When they complain about doing the dishes, "Try again."

When I ask them to take out the trash and they start whining about how they did it last time too, "Try again."

Even the teen with rolling eyes and exasperated sighs, having been forced to stay home and hang out with the family on a Saturday afternoon, knows what it means when her dad lovingly reminds her to, "Try again."

Sometimes in the middle of the afternoon when my children are ornery and I'm melting at the sink with a pile of dishes and a migraine too, we all need to start over and "Try again."

I remember the first time I discovered a refreshing variation of our familiar script. I turned from the dishes and asked my oldest to finish them while I took a cold shower and got some fresh clothes on.

"But you already took a shower today," he said.

"Yes, but I need a do-over."

"A what?"

"A do-over. I'm spent and tired and want to put your brothers to bed and call it a night, but it's only 1:17 in the afternoon, so I'm going to freshen up and try again."

Since then I've called a "do-over" for my children too. They know what it means when it's mid-morning and they're already having trouble on a gorgeous summer day. "Alright everyone," I've been known to say, "I want everyone to go brush their teeth and splash some water on their face before coming out again. I'm giving you a do-over. Let's see if we can press the restart button on our day and make it better."

At first they thought I was joking, but on homeschooling days especially, I sometimes take my middle boy by the hand and walk him to his sink. Do-overs are now a real and appreciated thing around our home.

When they're all jostling for the best seat on the couch, dangerously close to turning our family movie night into a family fight, I call out, "do-over!" They get up and go back to their rooms then try coming out again.

And isn't that grace? And aren't those words exactly what the Lord's new mercies look like in our own lives? Try again. Do over. Start fresh and clean, not so much because you've been washed by a cold shower, but because you've been washed by the blood of the lamb. That's the ultimate do over, and the reason we can respond gracefully to our children when they've done wrong, whether we're ready with a pre-planned script or not. Because we've known grace, we can give it. Because the Lord allows his children to "try again," with the help of His Holy Spirit, I can allow my kids to "try again" with my help.

Here at the end of our book we invite you to try again and again and again and again, if need be. As you take hold of each new mercy, every new morning, don't forget to take hold of the cross of Christ. That is where new mercies and enduring grace are available to us, morning by morning. And don't forget to take hold the Word of God. Each time you need to press the restart button, start there. The Bible is God's Word, and it is living and active and able to separate right from wrong—right responses from wrong reactions. As you intentionally choose your words be intentional to get into The Word.

Choose the Word as you choose your words.

Choose the Word as you choose your words.

The power to change ultimately isn't going to be found in this book, but in the good book. R. C. Sproul said it this way:

"I think the greatest weakness in the church today is that almost no one believes that God invests His power in the Bible. Everyone is looking for power in a program, in a methodology, in a technique, in anything and everything but that in which God has placed it—His Word. He alone has the power to change lives for eternity, and that power is focused on the Scriptures (R. C. Sproul, *The Prayer of the Lord*).

A double minded man cannot wield a double-edged sword. Be fully devoted to the renewing of your mind in God's transforming Word. It is never a waste of time! If you want to respond to sin in your home, like God in his gentleness responds to you, spend time with Him in His Word. If you want to bear the fruit of His Spirit in your home, abide with Him in His Word.

SCRIPT-URE:

"For the word of God is living and active, sharper than any two-edged sword, piercing to the division of soul and of spirit, of joints and of marrow, and discerning the thoughts and intentions of the heart"

(Hebrews 4:12)

PRAYER SCRIPT:

"Dear Lord, before I turn on them with correction, help me to turn to You! You are the parent I want to be. When I am short-tempered, You are long-suffering. When I am worn and weary, You are new mercies and grace. That's who I want to be. But how can I be like You unless I abide in You, and You abide in me, and Your Words become my words, my scripts? And so, Holy Spirit, I invite You, as I did in the very first chapter, to start with me. Me with You. From that intimate abiding place, deal with me. Transform me. And through the doorway of my own surrendered life, come into the lives of the other people in our home and deal with them. You are the One and only God over this family. In Jesus' gentle yet powerful name, amen."

MAKE THE SCRIPT YOUR OWN:

Have you fully invited God into your parenting? Have you yielded your life to Him and told Him that He is your God and welcome to help you script each word you speak? In the workbook pages, write your own prayer, giving Him full access to your heart and home, to your faith and your family, in your words and in your tone. He can have it all.

Workbook Pages —

_____

_____

_____

_____

_____

_____

_____

_____

_____

_____

_____

_____

_____

_____

_____

_____

_____

_____

_____

_____

_____

_____

_____

_____

_____

_____

_____

_____

_____

_____

_____

_____

_____

_____

_____

_____

_____

_____

_____

_____

_____

_____

_____

ACKNOWLEDGEMENTS

Brooke McGlothlin, Erin Mohring, Lori Mercer, Sandra Peoples, Trena Turner, and the rest of the MOB Society team— Thank you for all of the ways you have partnered with us to minister to families with the Gospel of Jesus Christ.

Pastor Bryan Pruett, thank you so much for reviewing *Parenting Scripts* with the Gospel in mind. Your words both affirmed and challenged us as we worked on this book to keep Jesus as our central focus.

WENDY SPEAKE:

God - I love you, because You first loved me. And I love others because I love You. Thank you for making it so simple, this life of faith.

Caleb, Brody, and Asher - We already dedicated this entire book to you on one of the very first pages. However, let me say it again here: You have all been so generous with me, perhaps you most of all Caleb Brunner, for you are my guinea pig. Gently loving and encouraging you boys is my true heart's desire, but doing it takes the Holy Spirit's abiding help each day. I'm learning, and as I learn, we learn together. What a privilege it is to learn gentleness and love by your side. Thank you again for allowing me to write and speak to families, pointing their hearts as I do yours to our Savior, Jesus Christ.

Matt - Your support means the world to me. From your strong arms, to your steady beating heart, to your admirable work ethic and the way you faithfully provide for our family, you support us. But this year especially you grew to support me in new ways—sending me out to love on families beyond our own. That's hard on you at times; I recognize that. Thank you for the sacrifice. If there's any eternal reward as a direct result of this work, I share it with you, Beloved.

Amber Lia - There are words I speak and ways I serve my family that I learned directly from you. That's profound to me as we wrap up another book together, Amber. I am better than I once was because of you, and I know there are many others who say the same. Yes, you make me better. Thank you for being my partner in all of this.

Amber Rogers, Kelli Stuart, and Angie Mosteller - I am overwhelmed by the love that the Lord has shown me in giving me such steadfast and wise, prayerfully devoted friends. Thank you for your faithfulness to our friendship. I am not a lonely woman; I have the dearest friends.

Alle McCloskey - You are so much more than a brand manager, you are a sister to be sure. I have no doubt the Lord gave you to me as a sincere gift, for He loves me! Thank you for helping me to navigate all of the good works the Lord has prepared for me. You keep me faithfully plodding forward.

Bethany Hockenbury – Your love for good writing pales only next to your love of people. I am so blessed to be one of your people. Thank you for your willingness to help make my words better.

AMBER LIA:

Guy Lia - We have always been a team and if it wasn't for you, this book would never have been written. You give me the time and space (and earplugs) I need to obey my calling, and I never take that for granted. I can't imagine parenting with someone who was not on the same page as me. Thank you for embracing a loving and gentle approach to fatherhood that mirrors and complements what I believe about motherhood. Together, we have embraced our "testoster-home," and together we will continue to be faithful to God's good gifts, our sons.

Oliver, Quinn, Oakley, and Quade - You have been so respectful to me as I took the time to write this book. You are so proud of me, and that makes my heart so happy. Thank you for being the very best boys I could ever ask for. You are my favorites! And not just because of your collection of freckles and your dimpled smiles, but because you have hearts that look a lot like Jesus' heart. I wouldn't trade you boys for all the world. Mommy loves you acres and oceans and buckets and barrels full! And that's quite a lot!

Wendy Speake - Sure, you are my writing partner. My sister in Christ. My friend. But you are also a mentor and a model of how to live out the Fruit of the Spirit as a mother. There is no script to express my gratitude for that, because words fail. I hope, instead, that you can feel it—my immense thankfulness for all that you are and for all that you have helped shape me to be.

Joanne Ferrilstone - Oh, the joy of having a soul sister who prays for me continually and champions me consistently. I truly don't know what I would do without you. I know that motherhood was not your path physically, but you have displayed the heart of a mother to so many, including me. Thank you for knowing my heart and for loving me through thick and thin.

Lord Jesus - The battle we fought in the spiritual realm to write this book was nothing short of breath-taking and soul-quaking. I was weak, so You made me strong. Thank You for using me. I'll never understand how You can take my desires and do more than I ask or imagine, but I'll never stop praising You for doing so. The glory is Yours.

CPSIA information can be obtained
at www.ICGtesting.com
Printed in the USA
LVHW041438161218
600666LV00017B/427/P